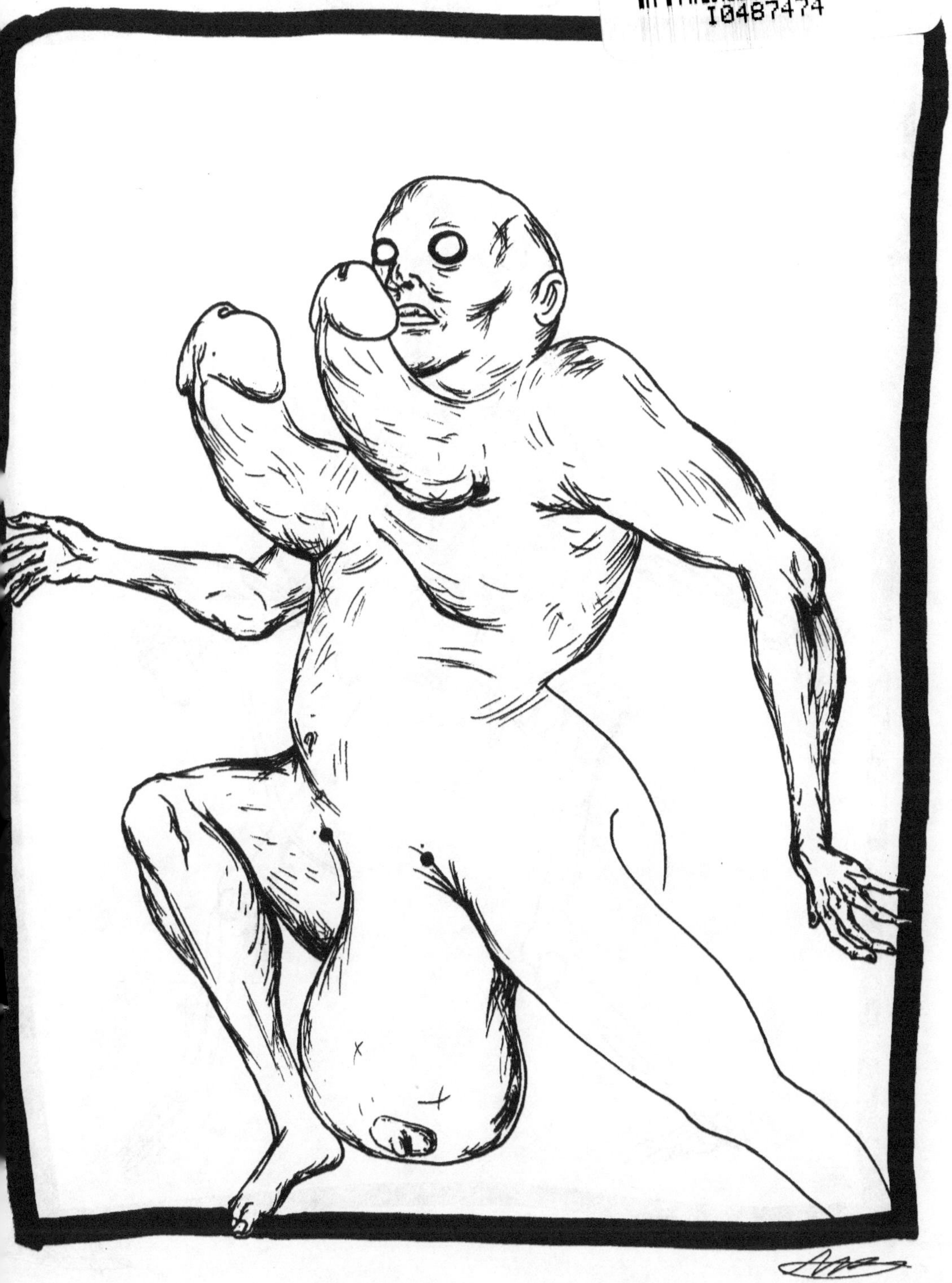

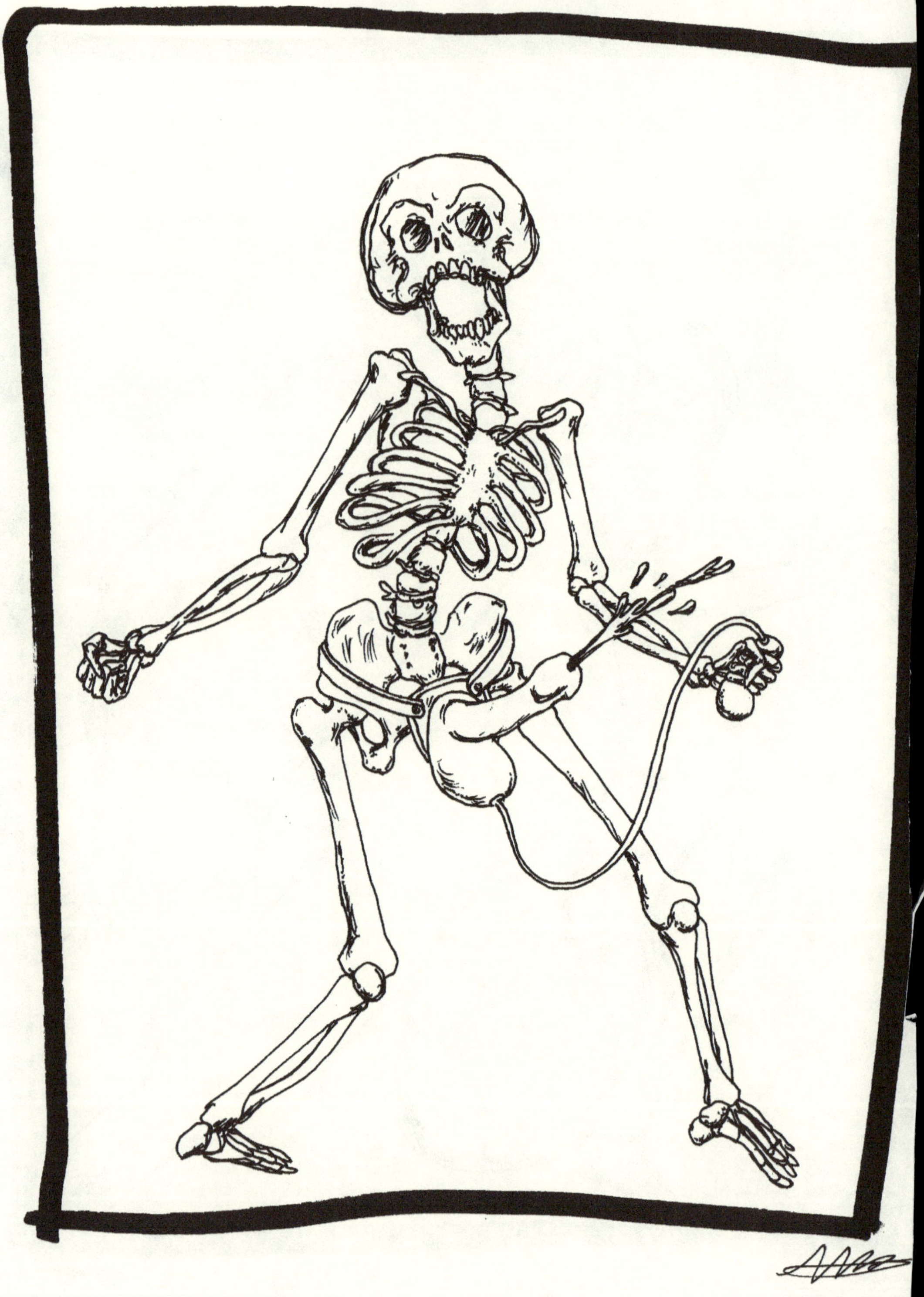

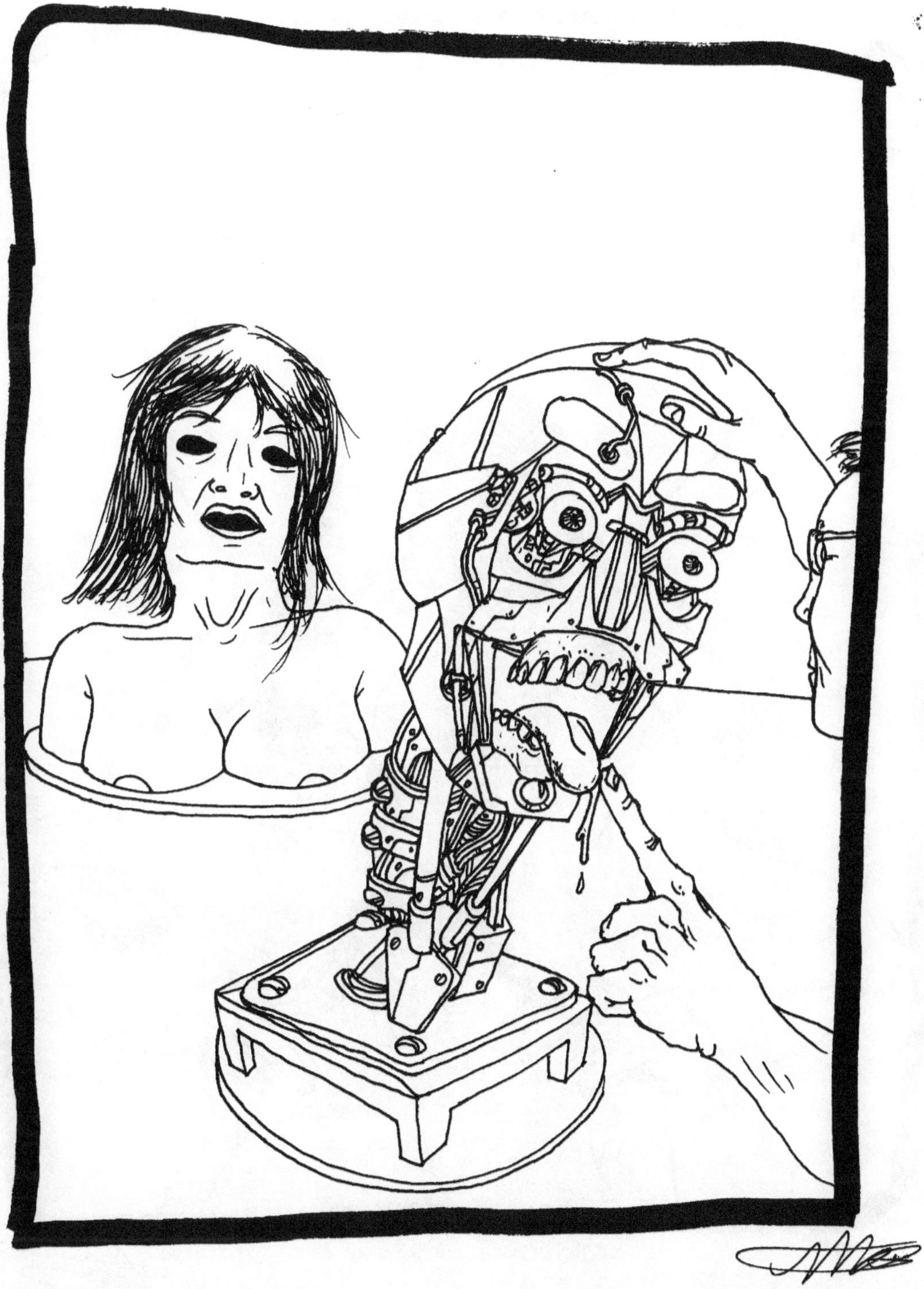

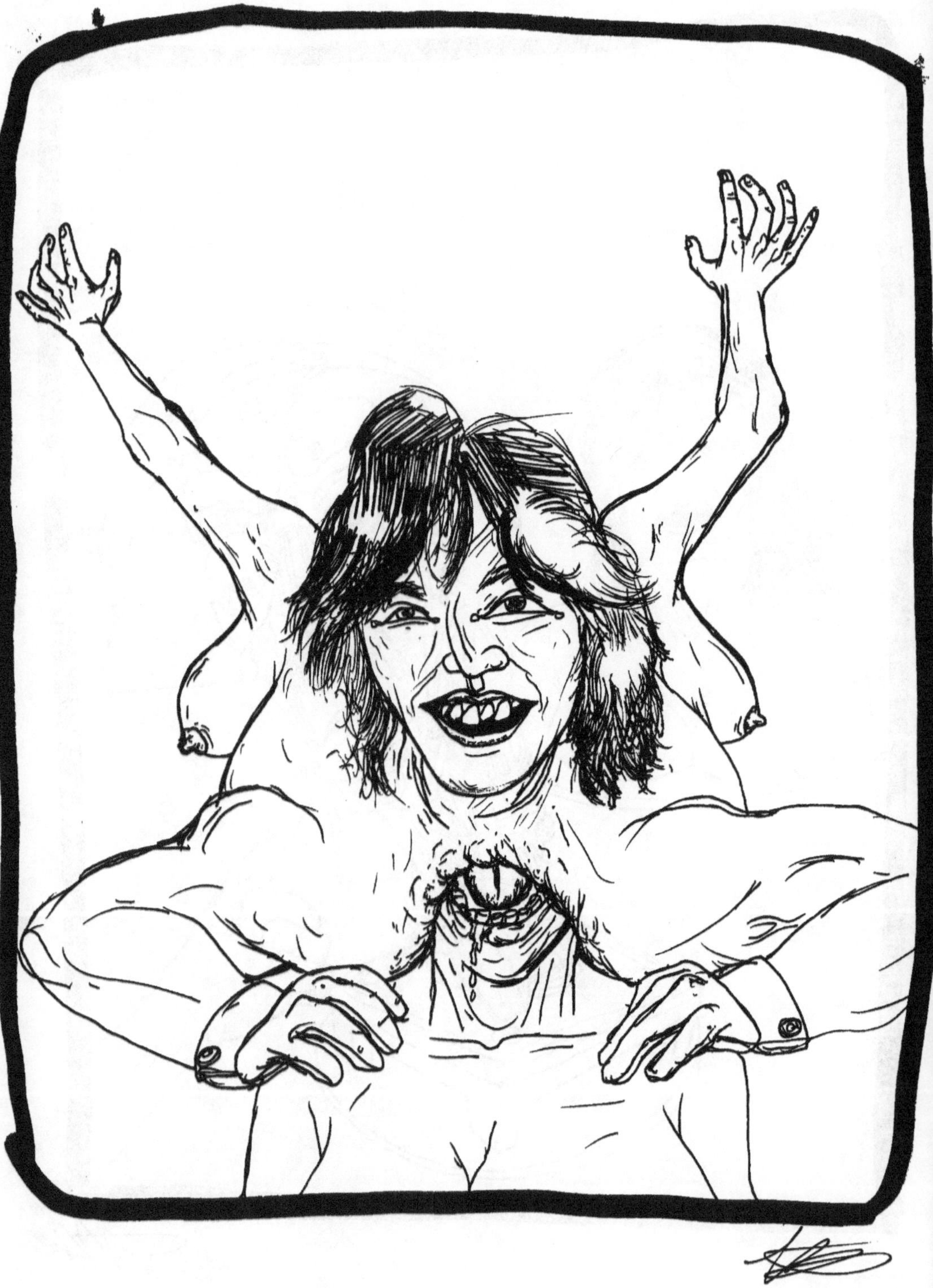

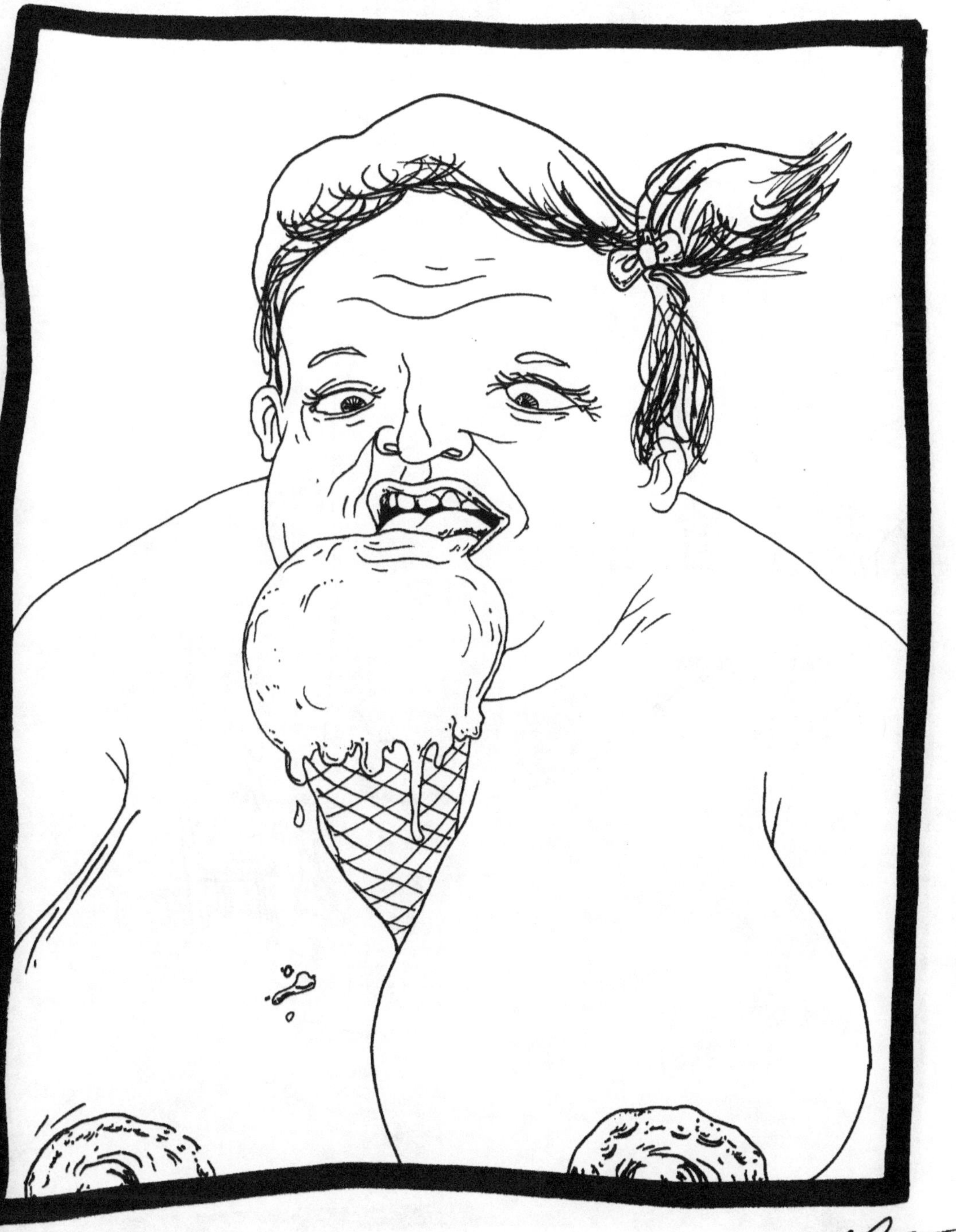

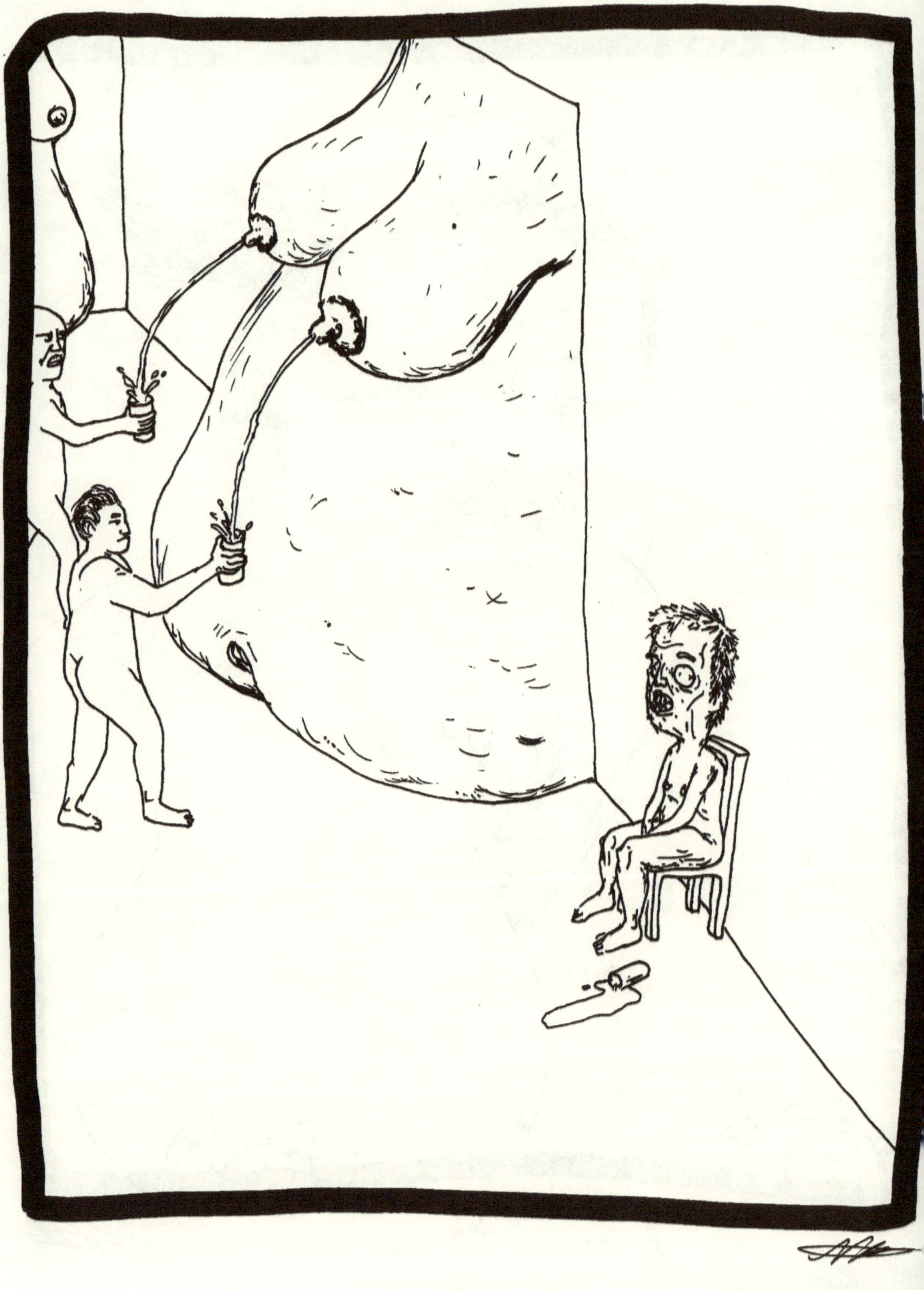

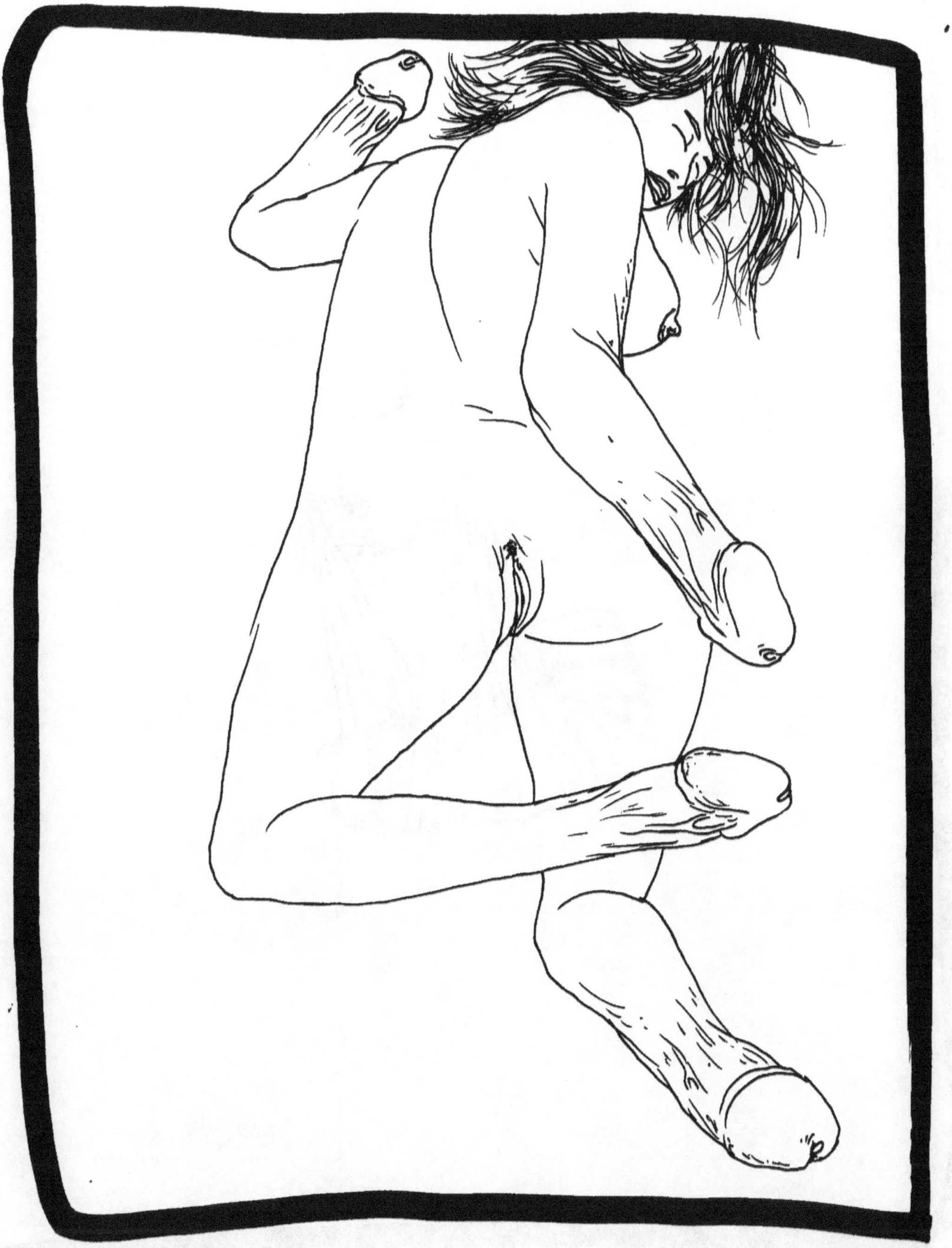

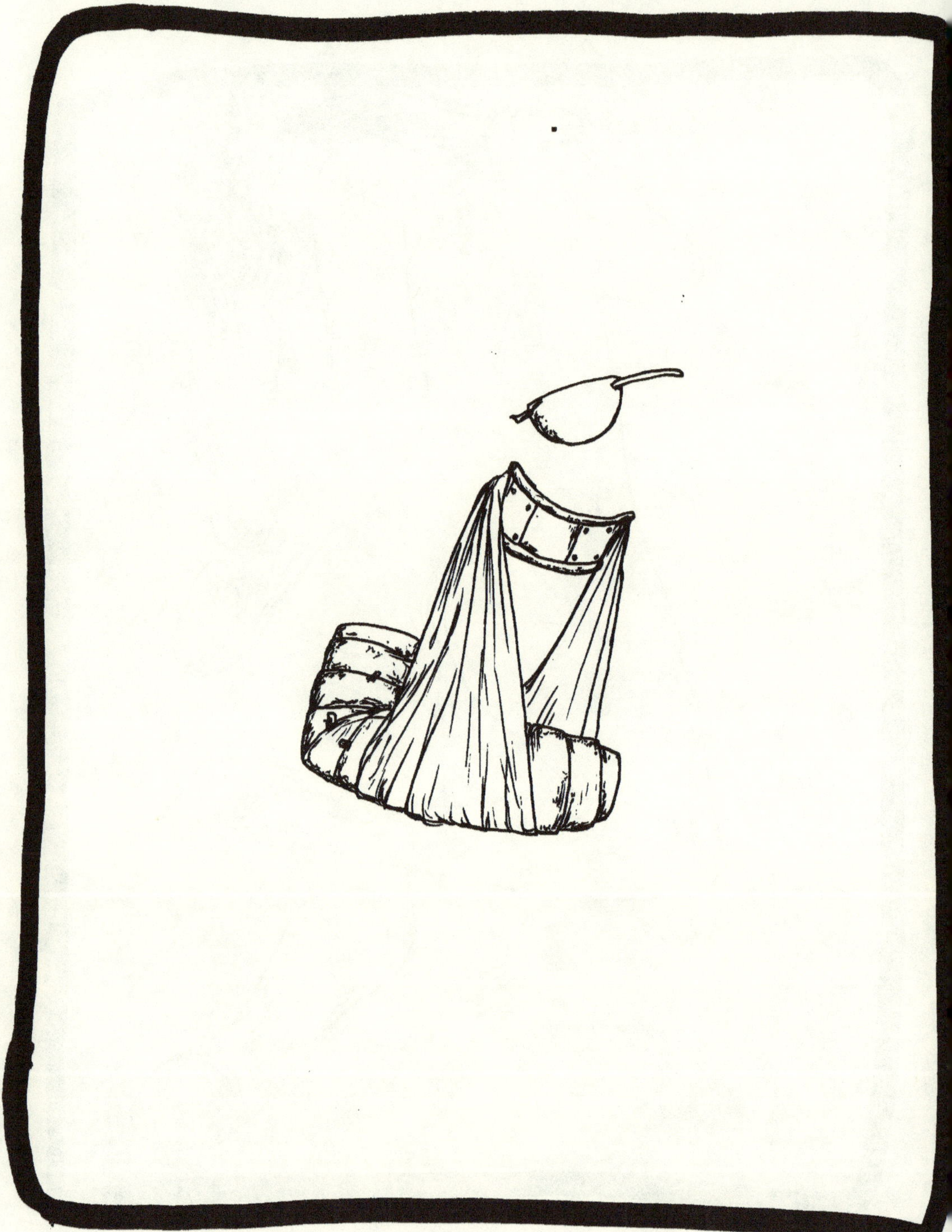

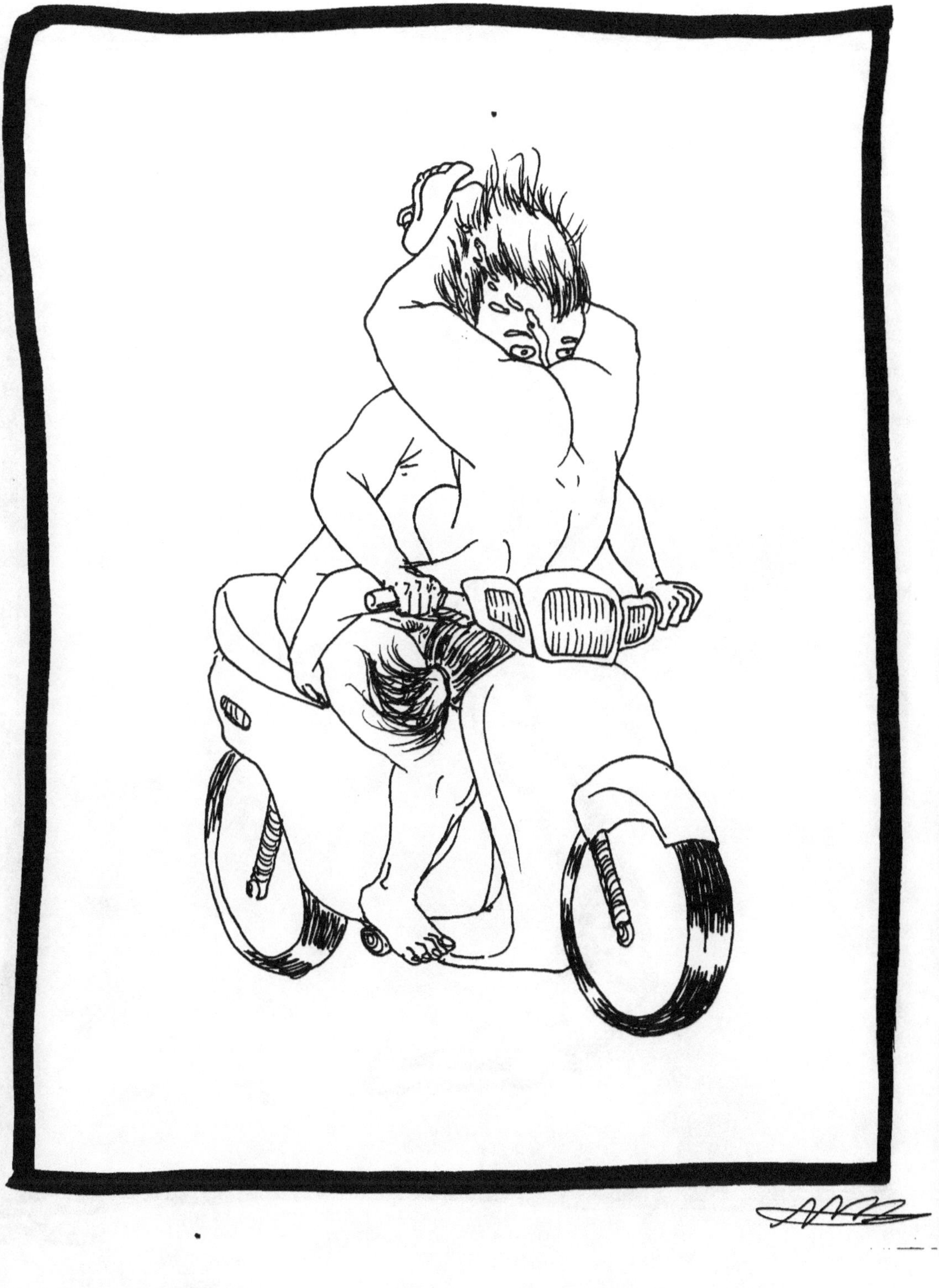

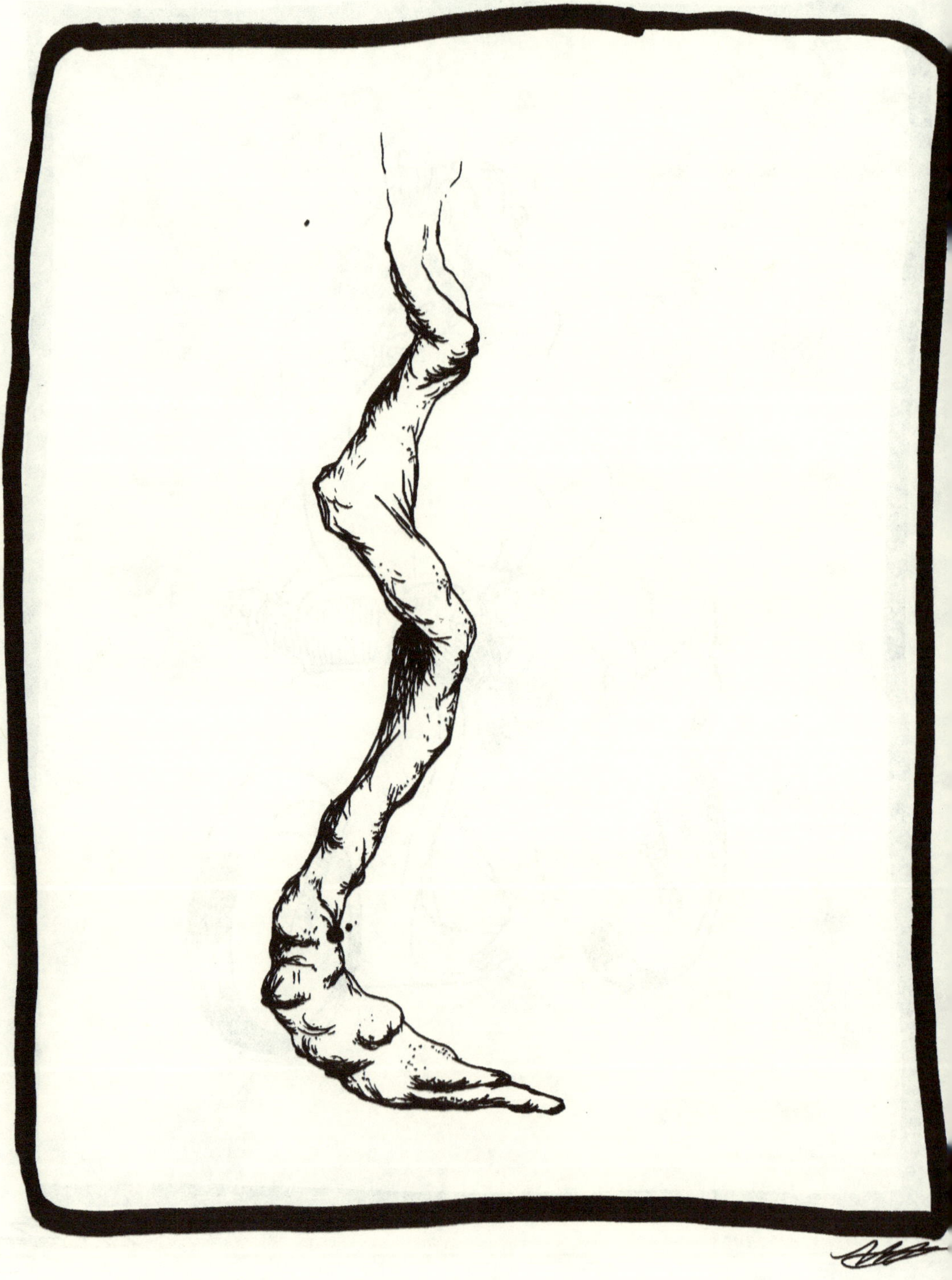

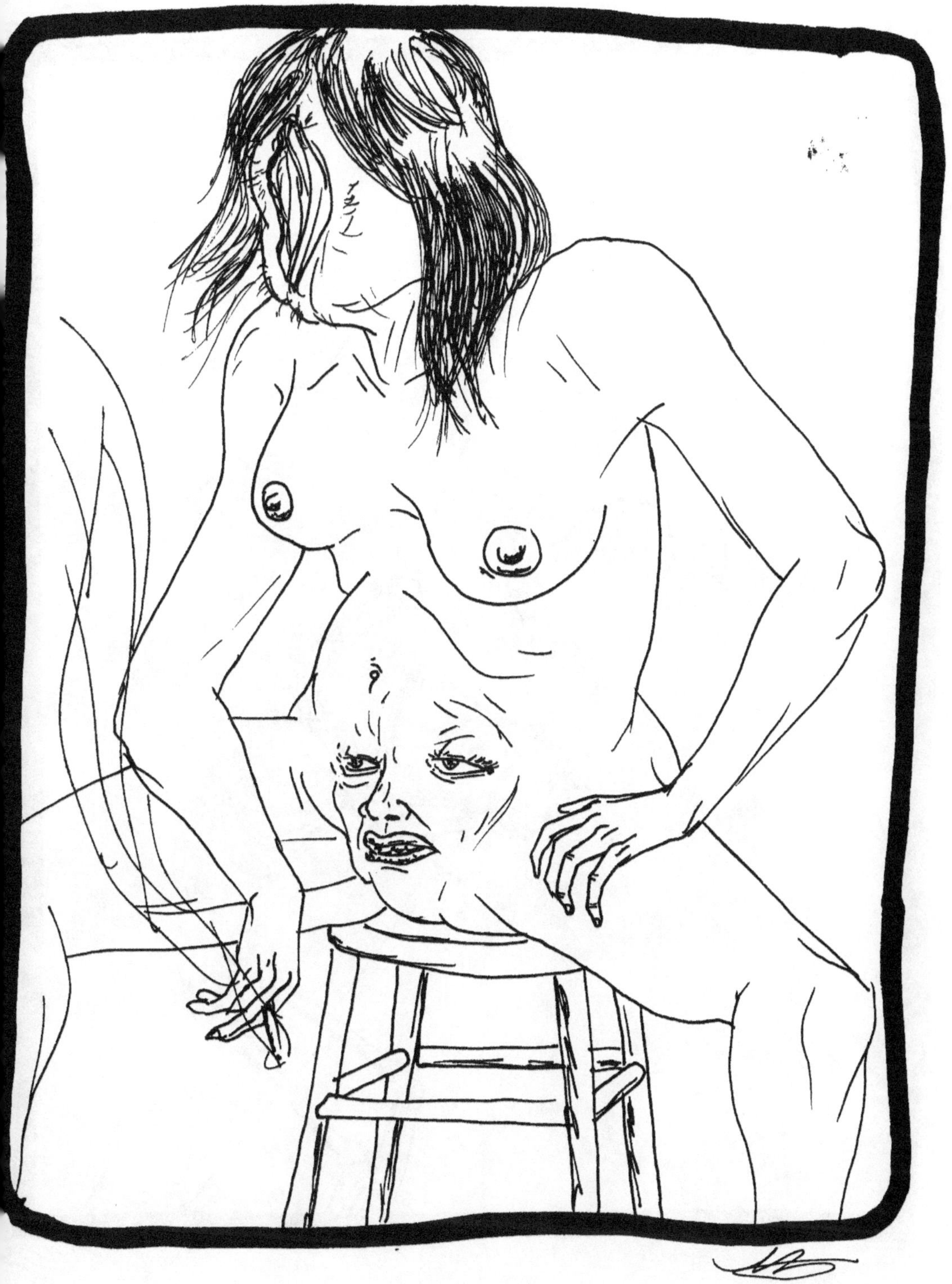

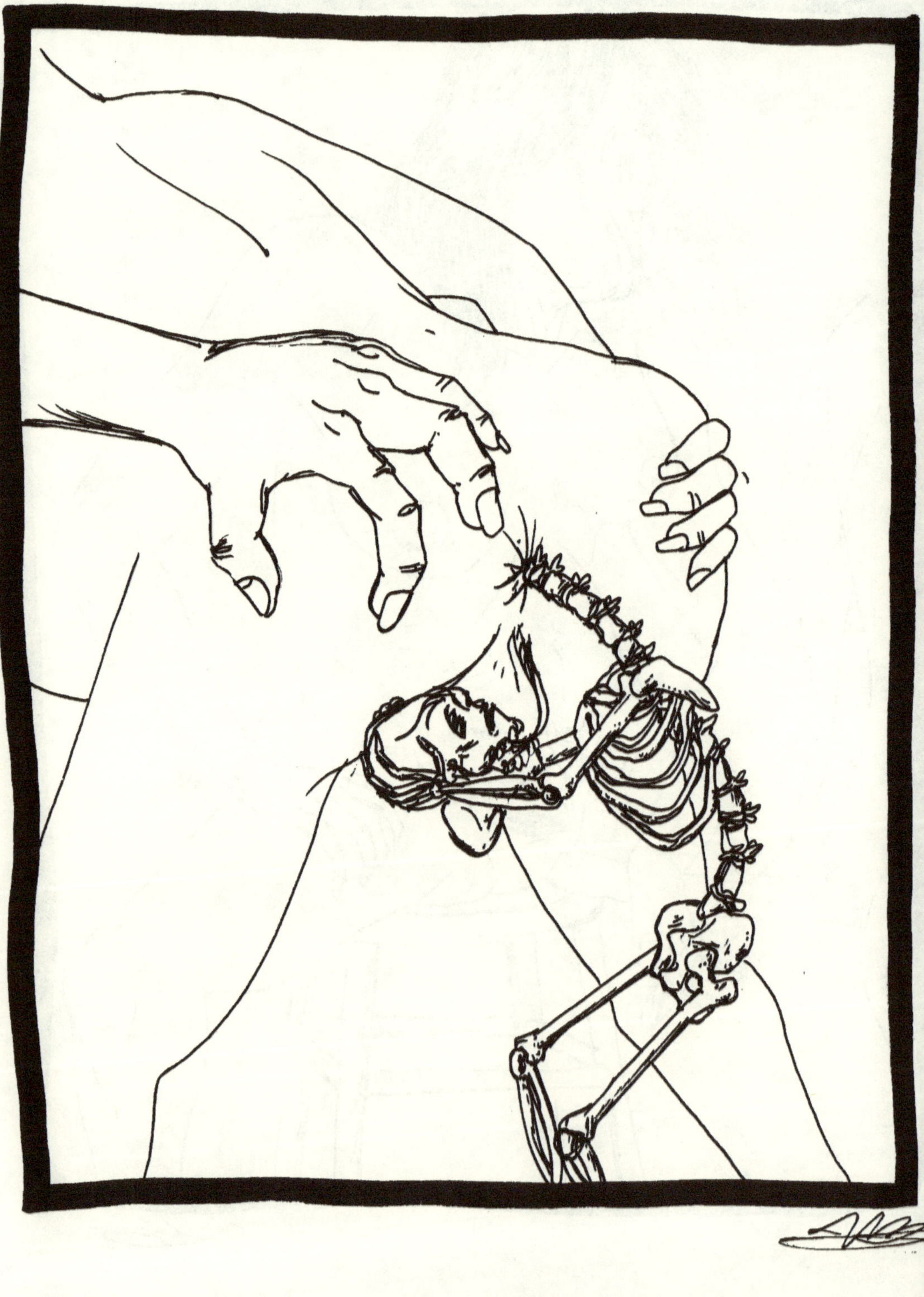

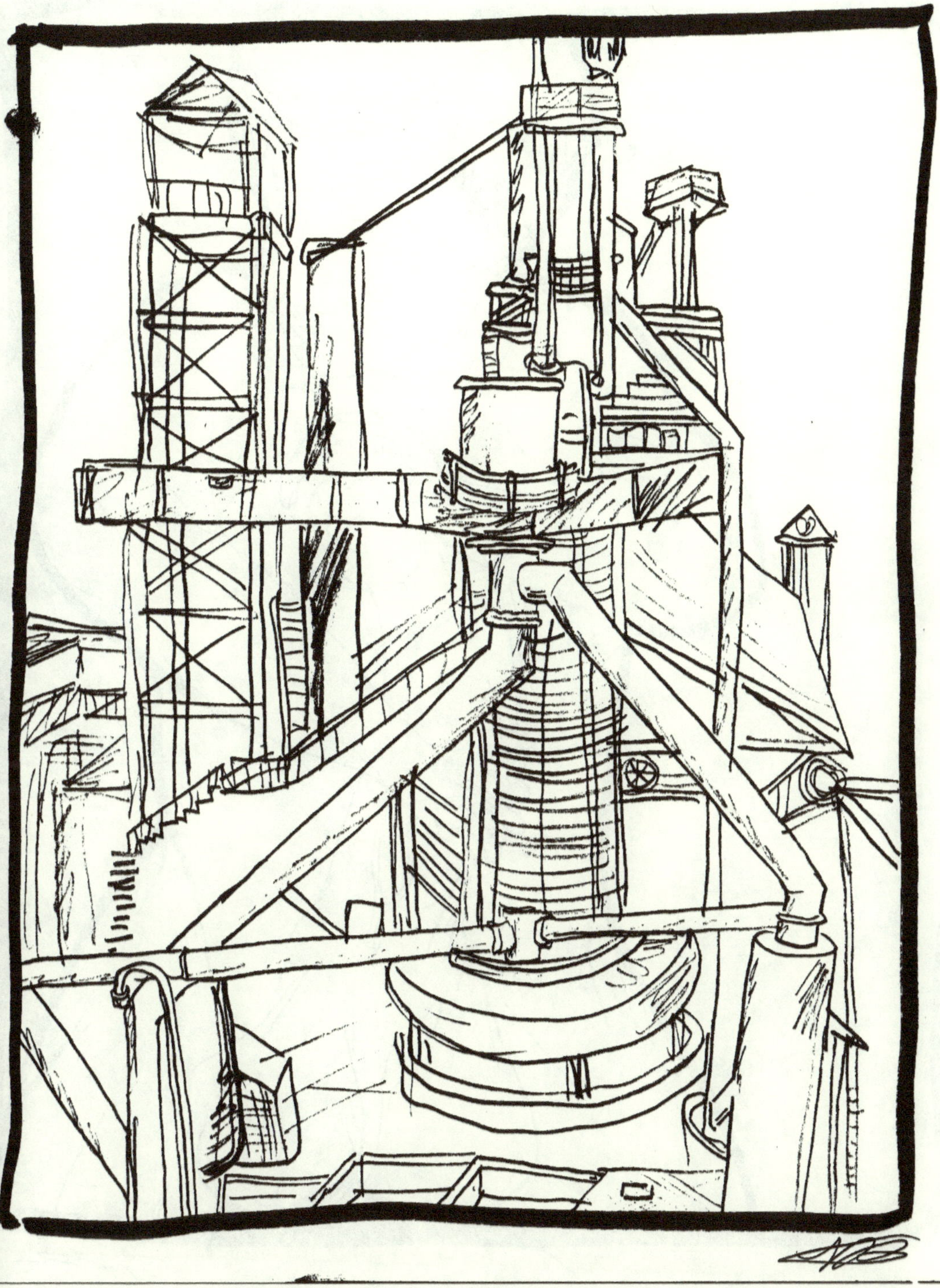

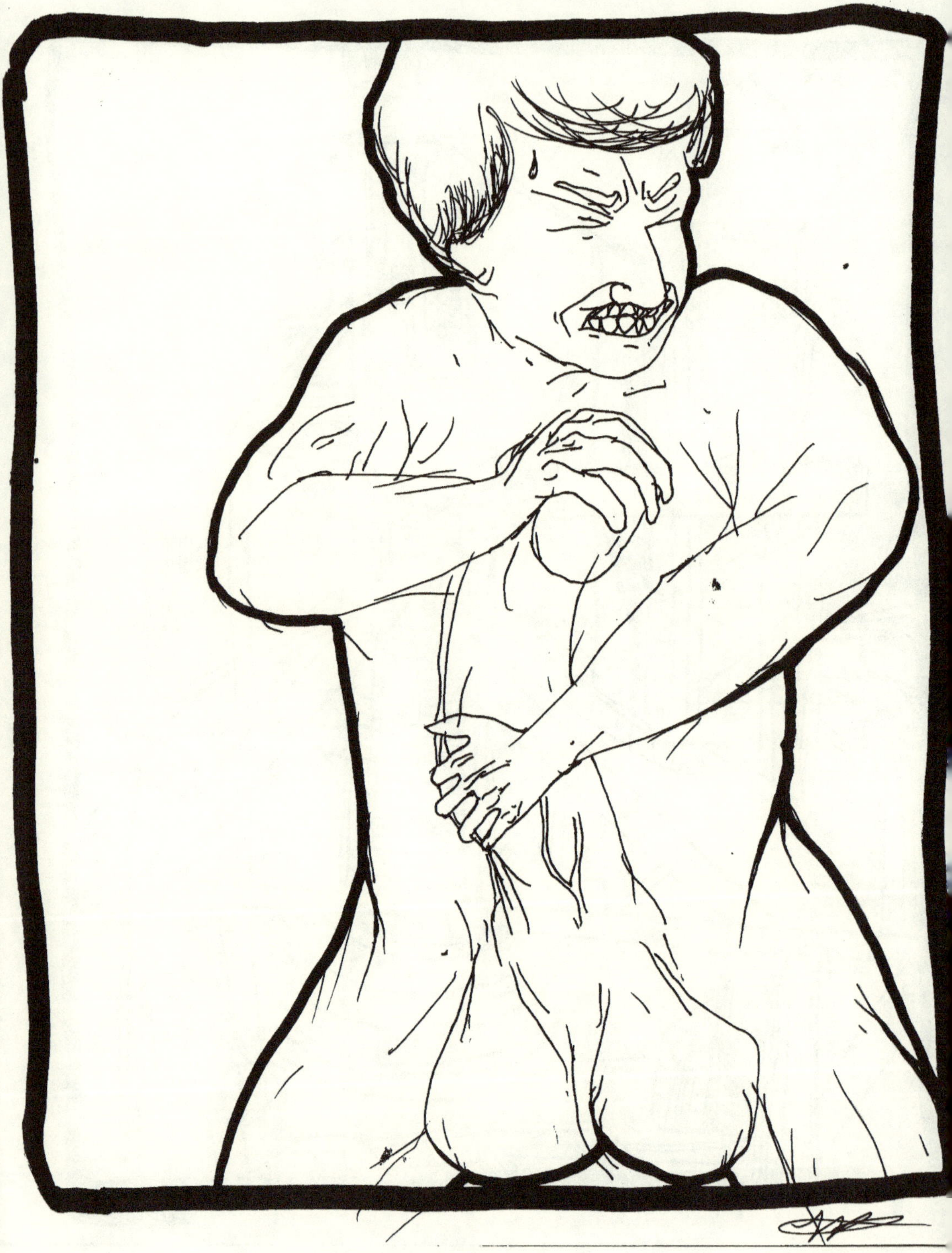

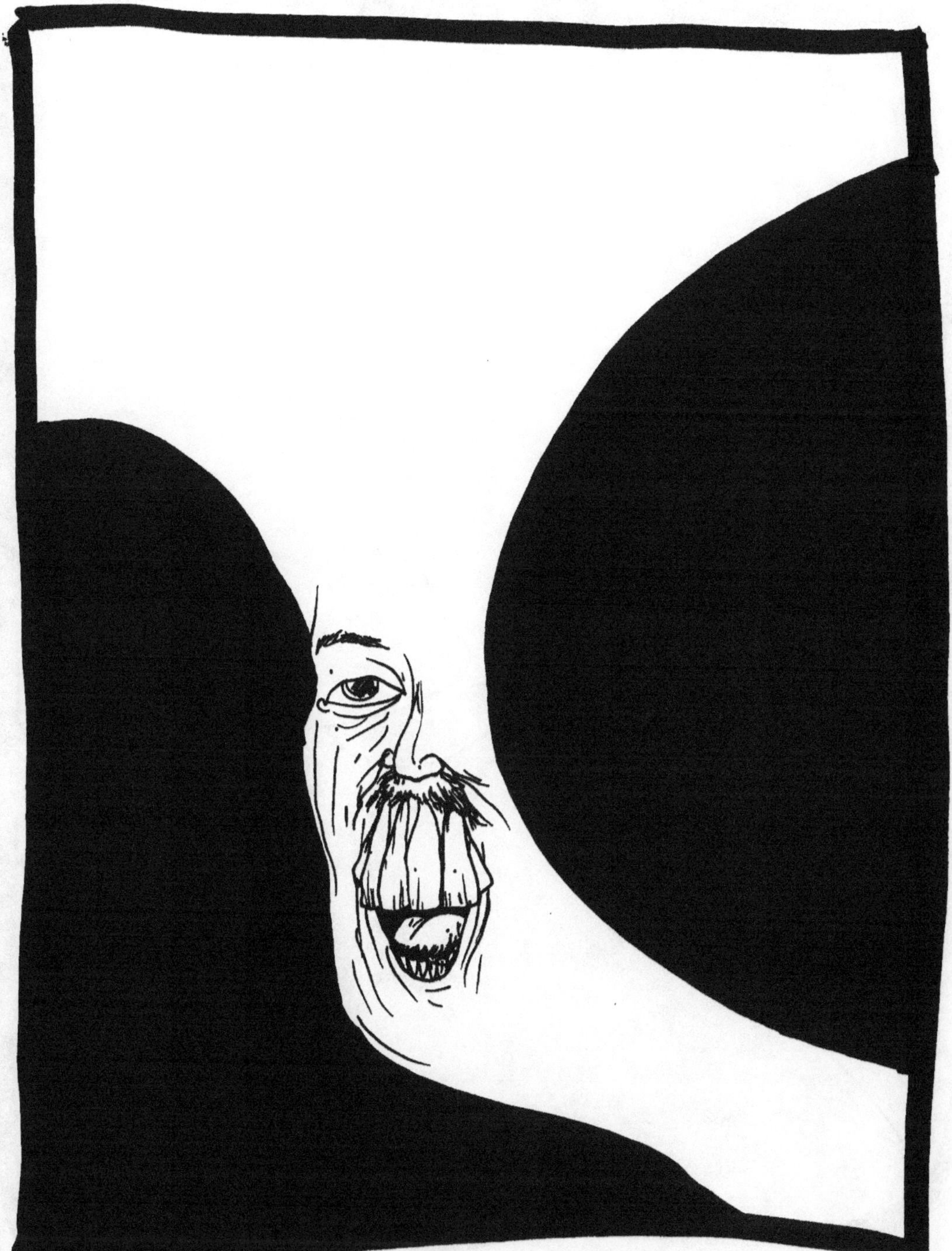

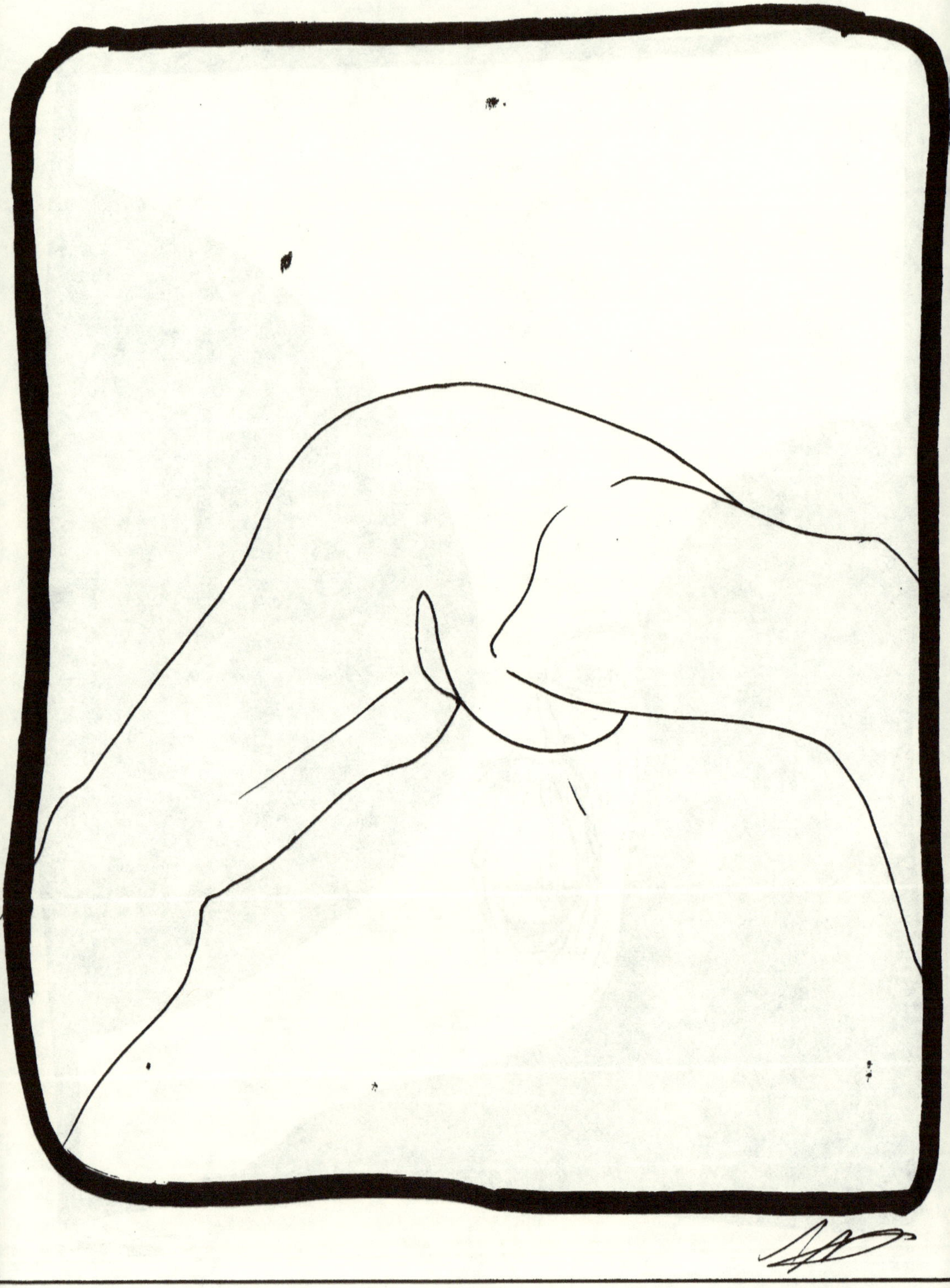

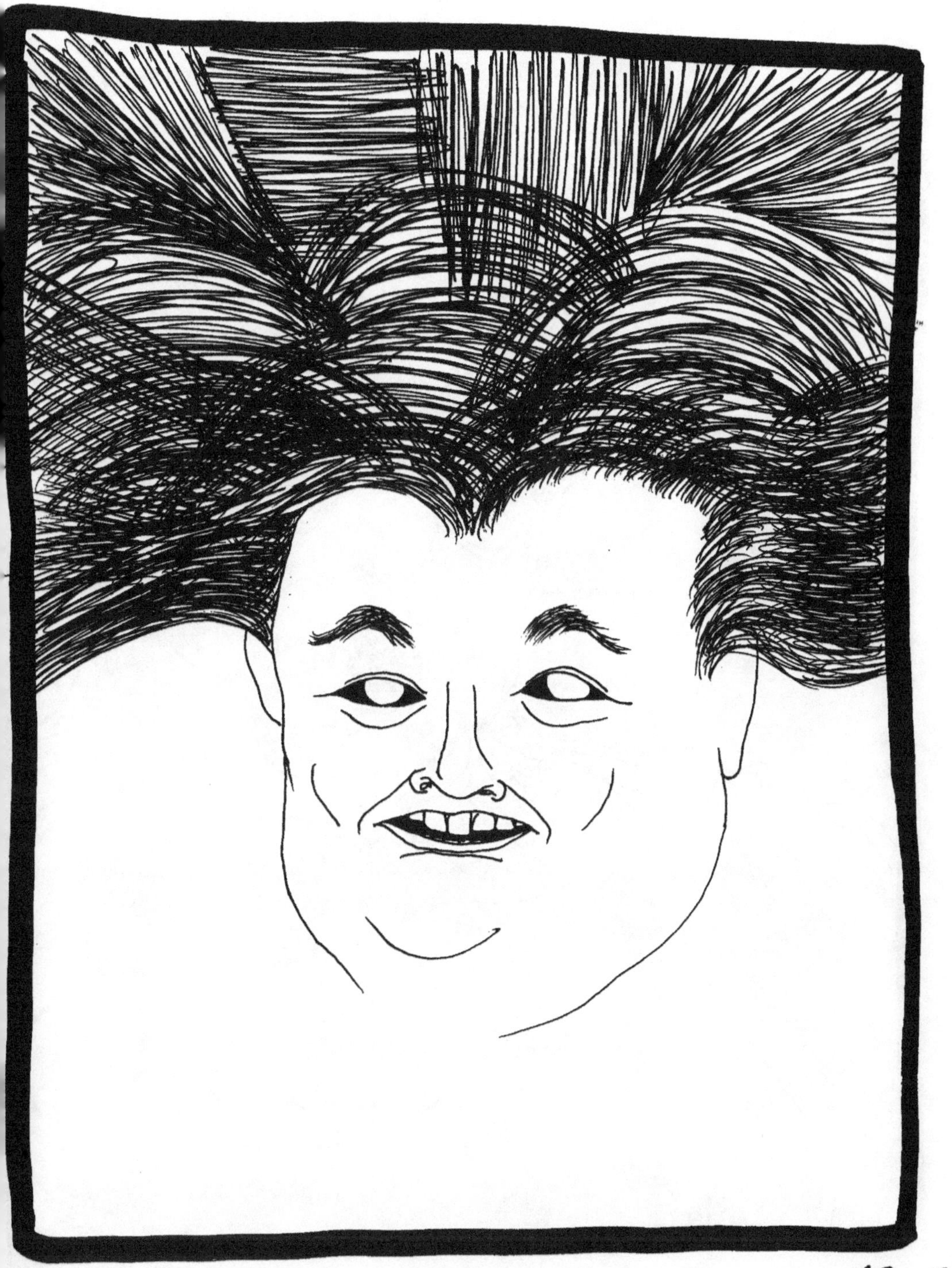

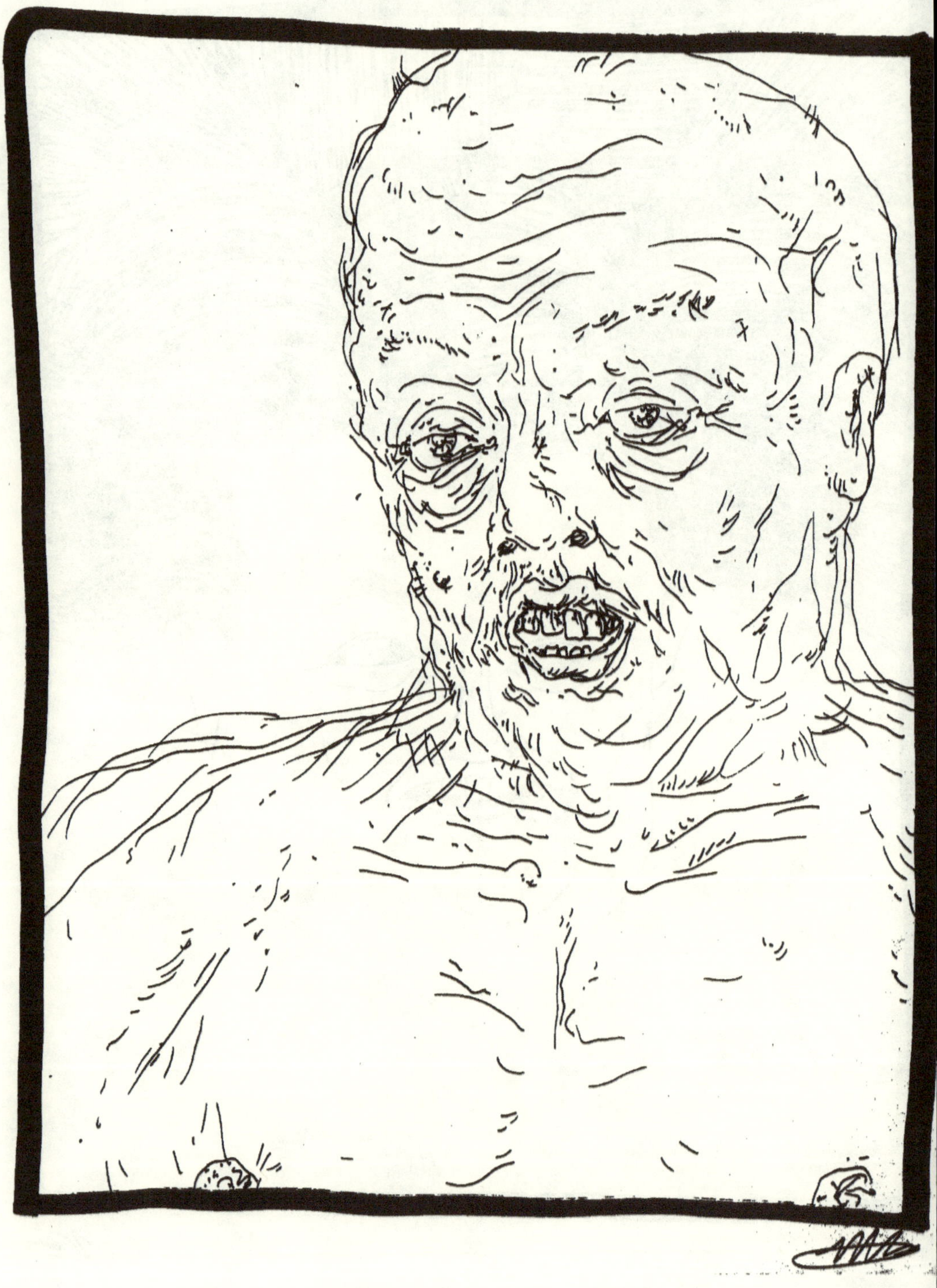

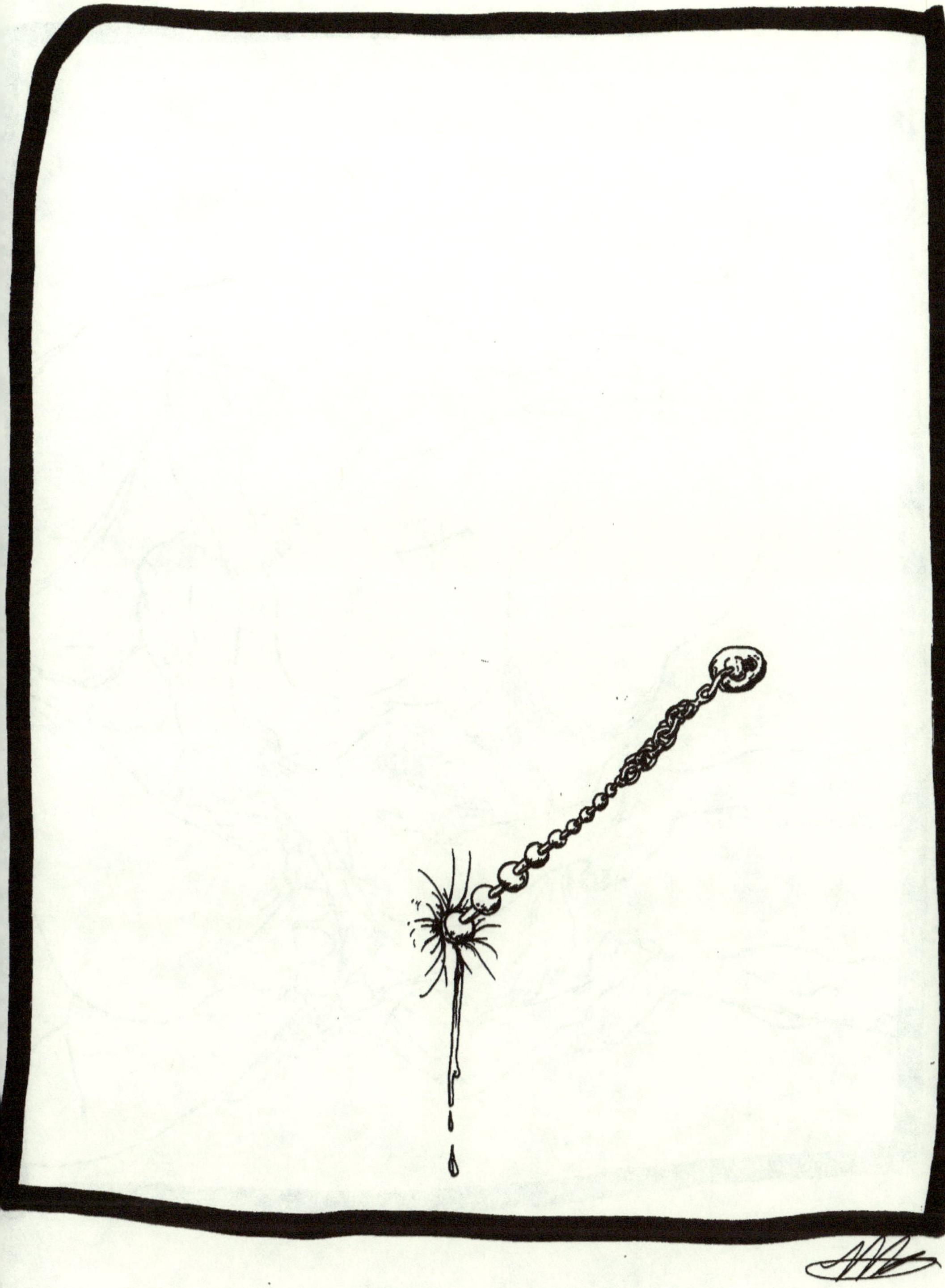

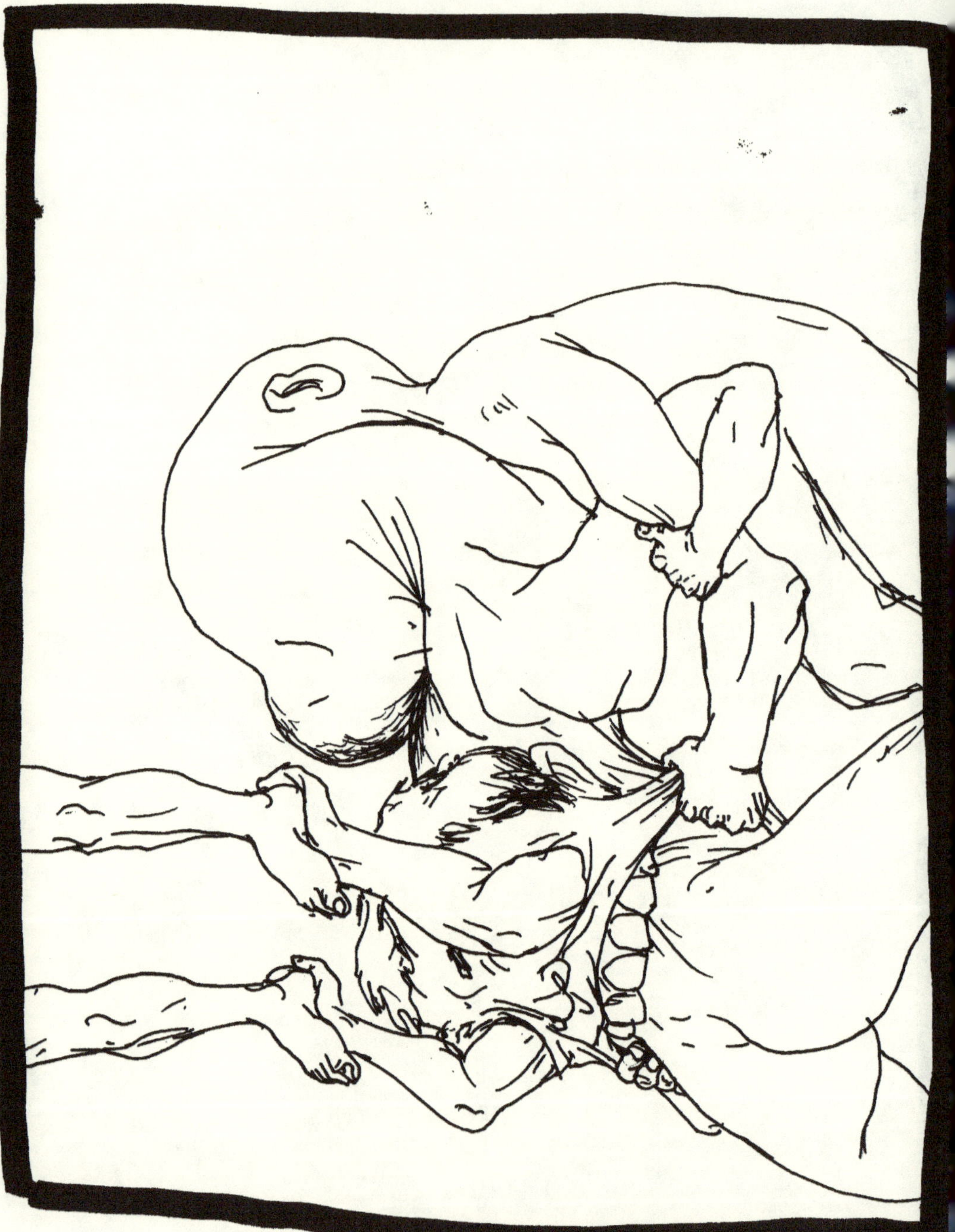

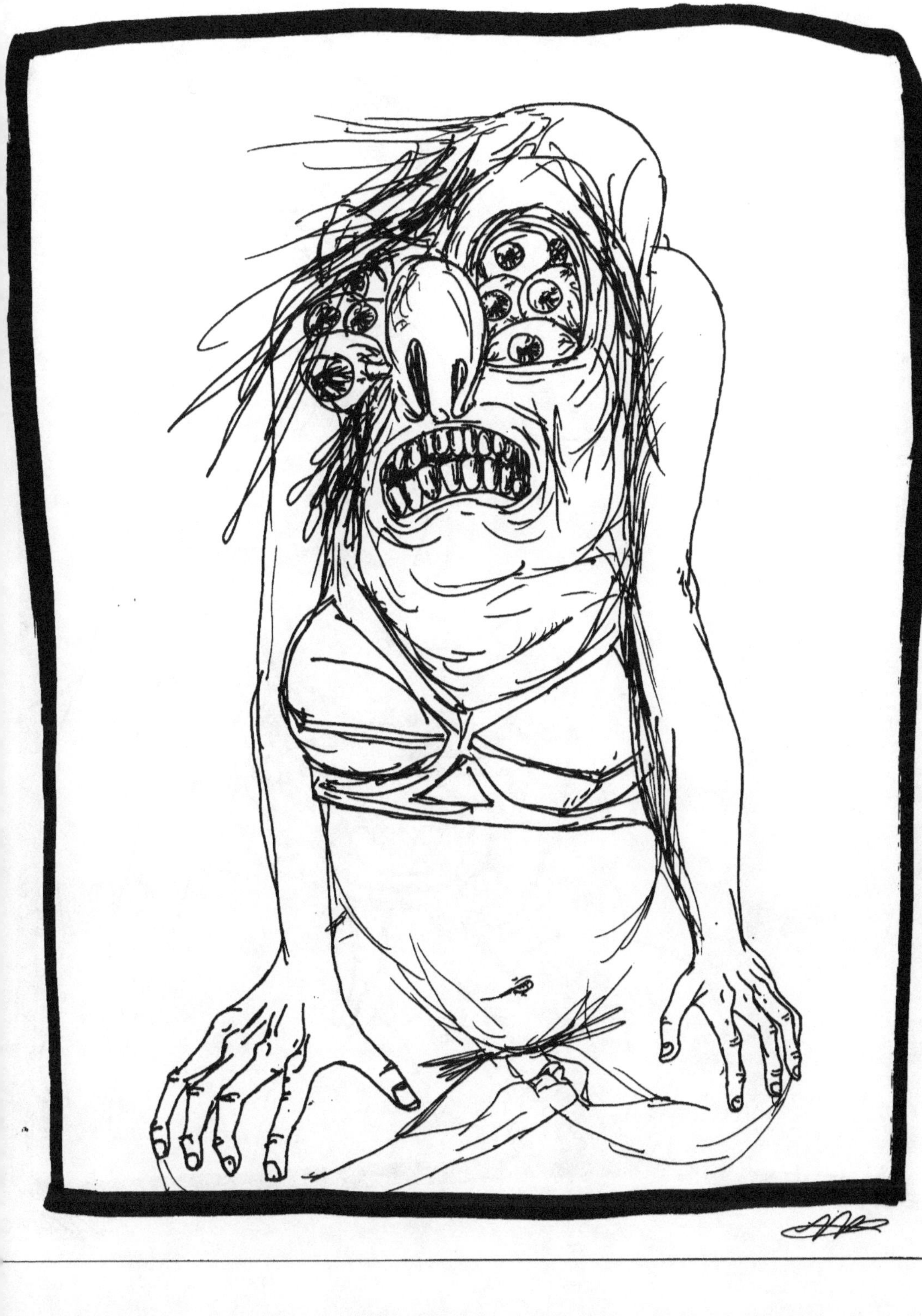

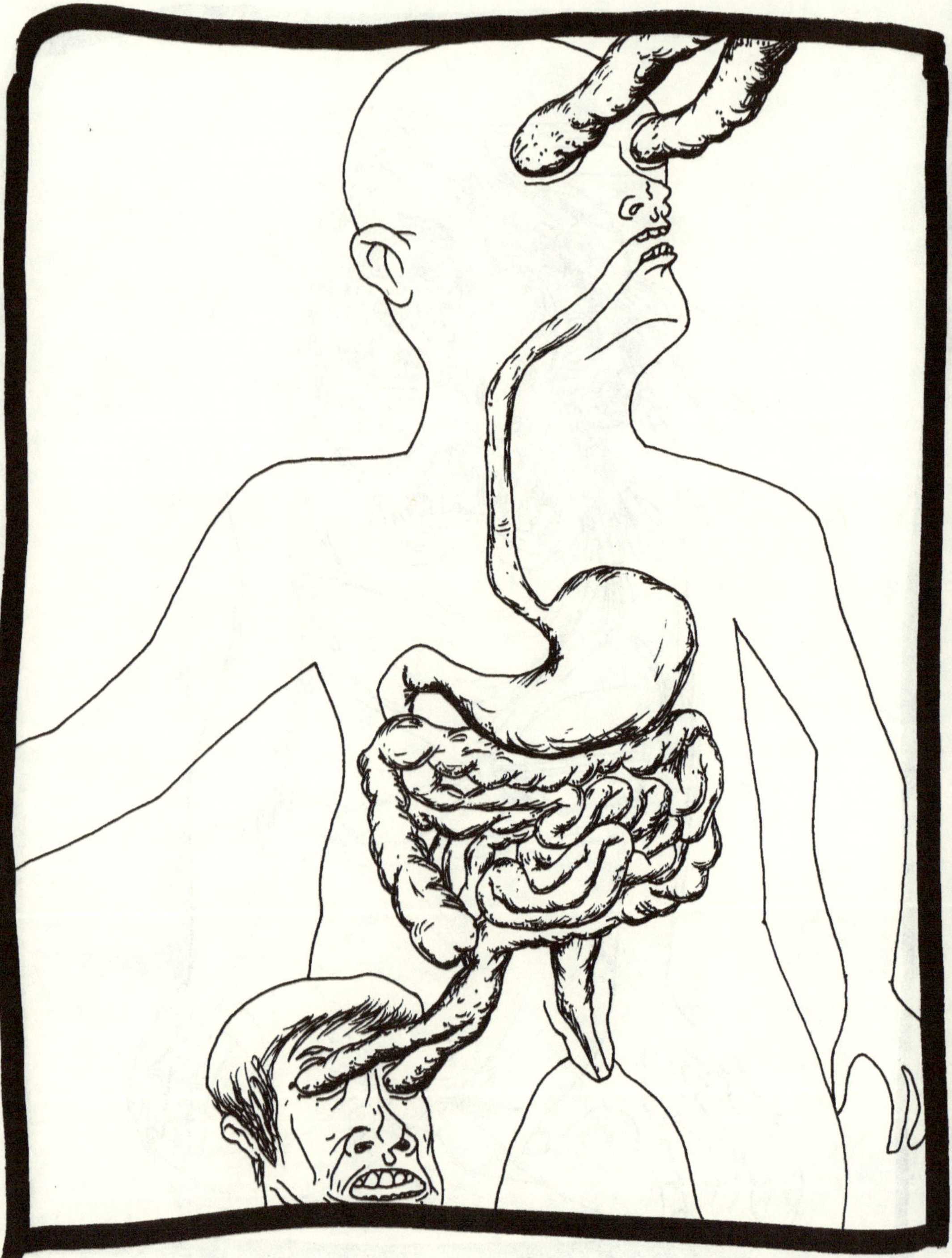

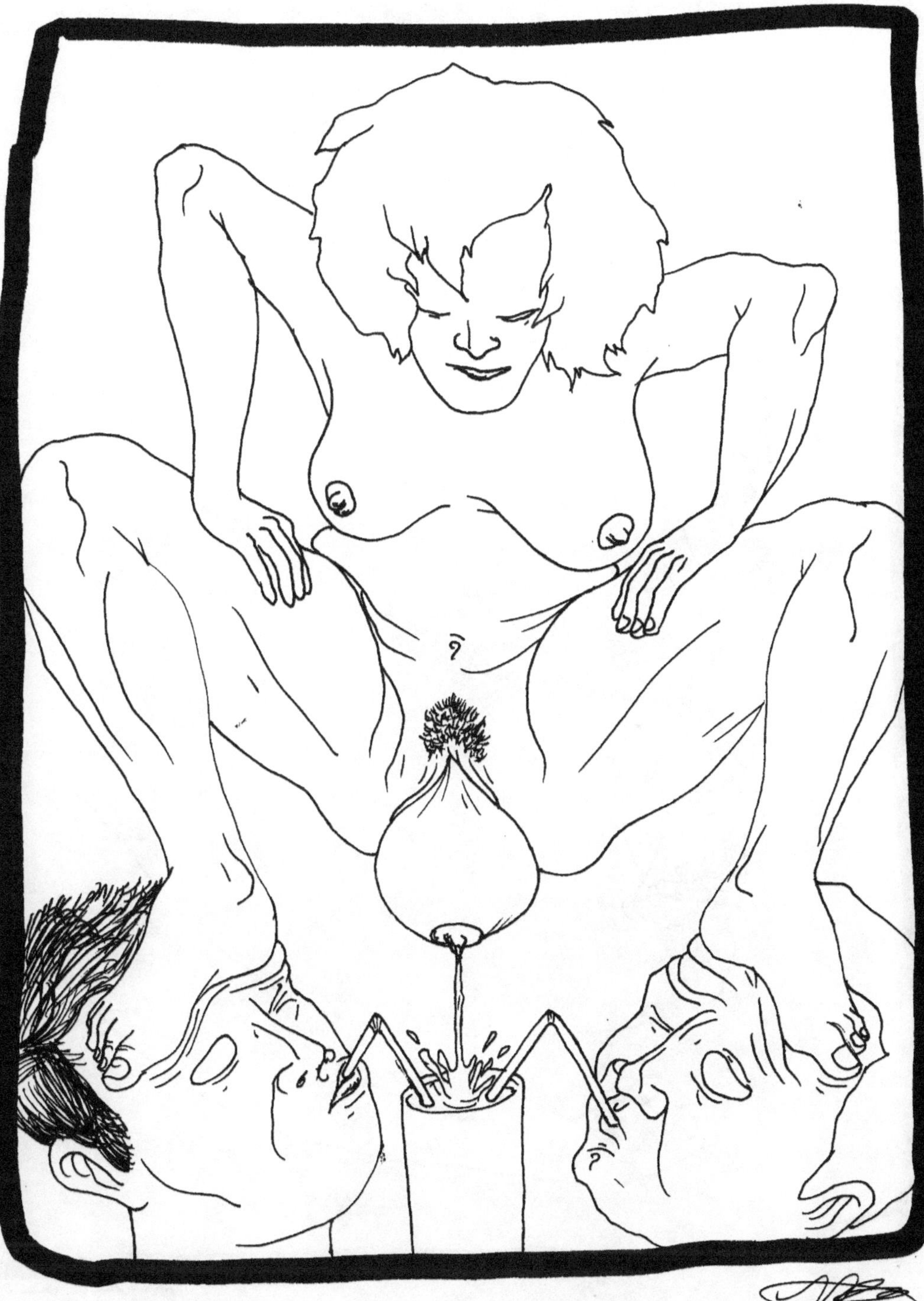

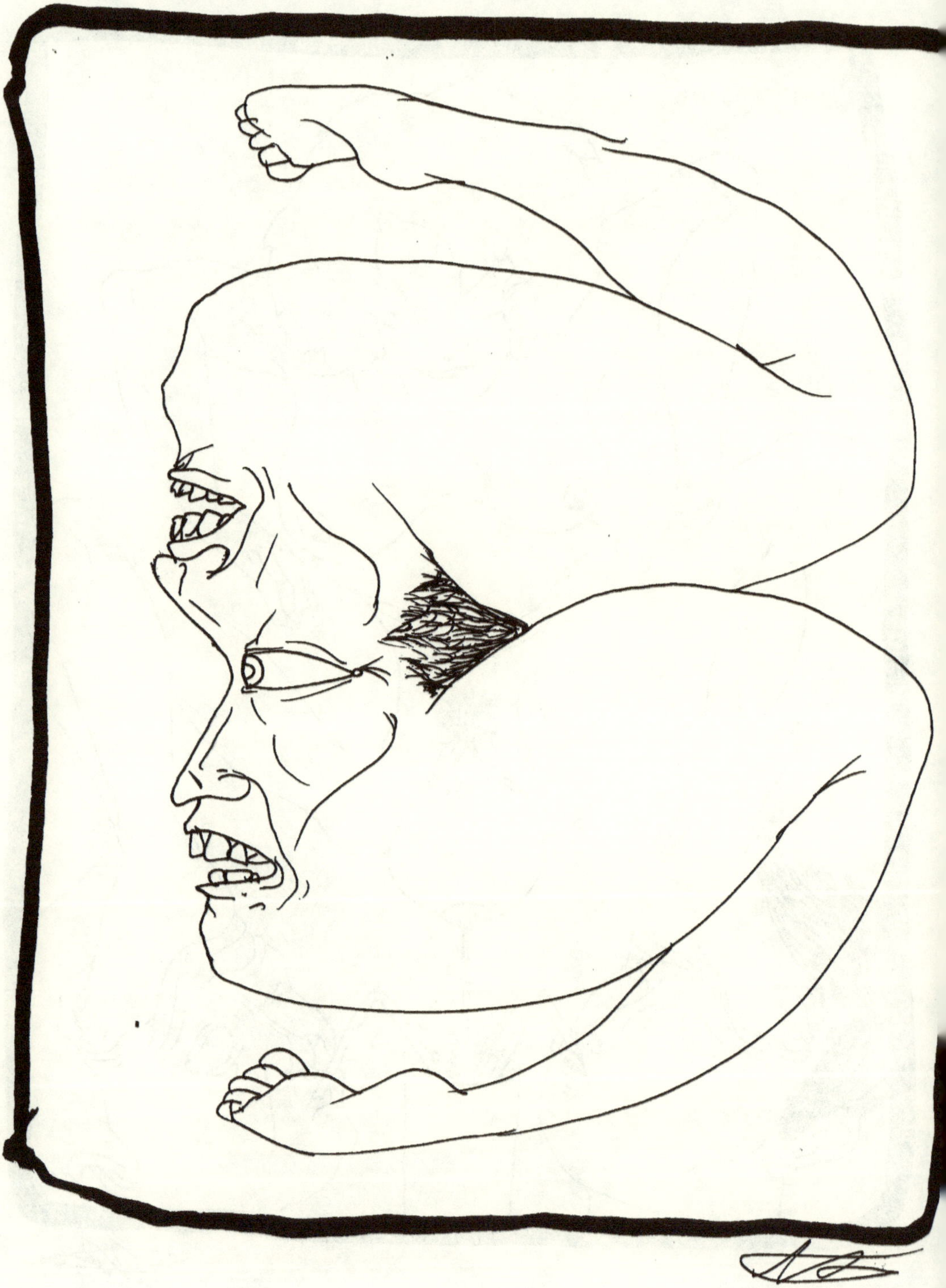

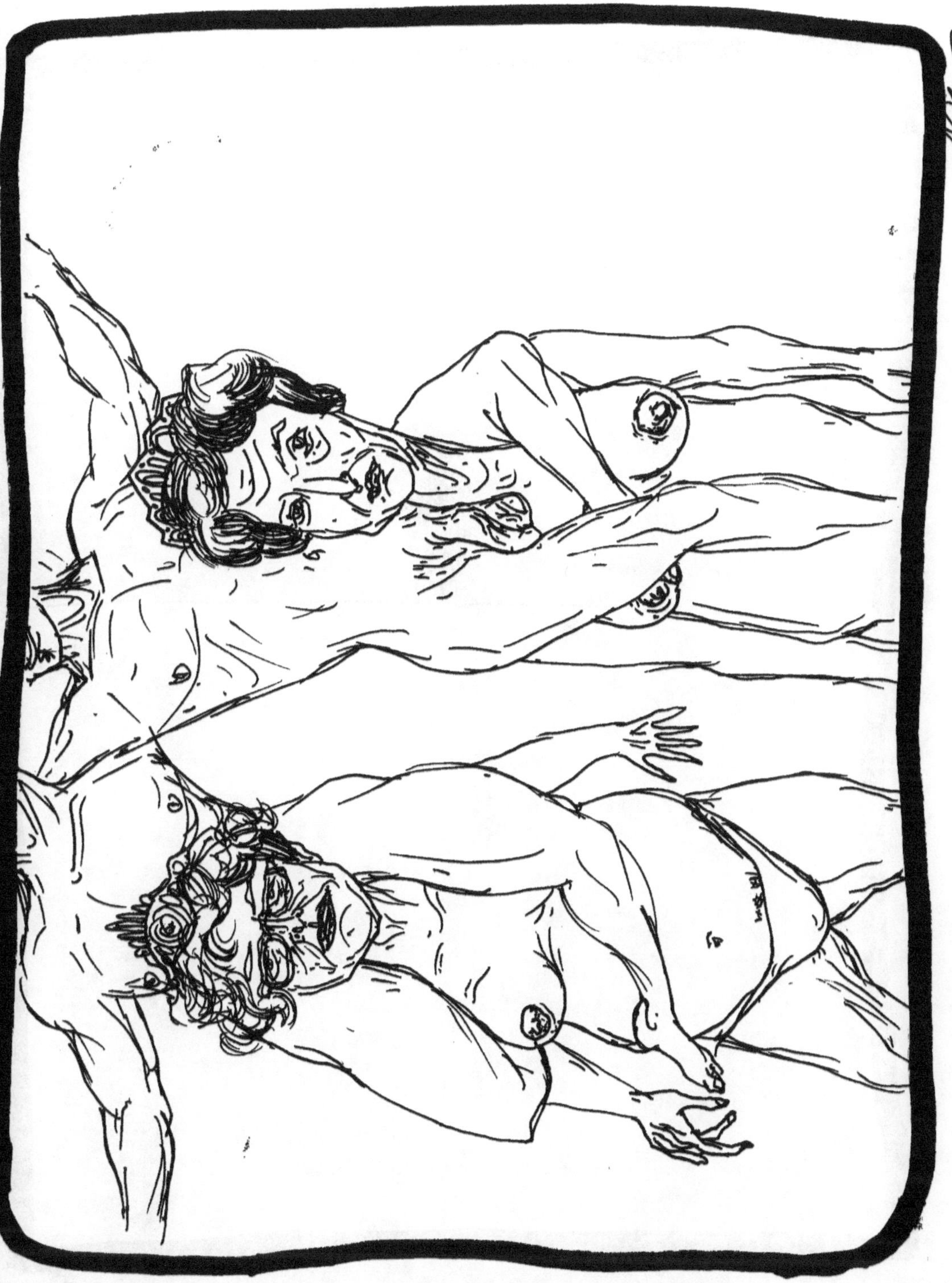

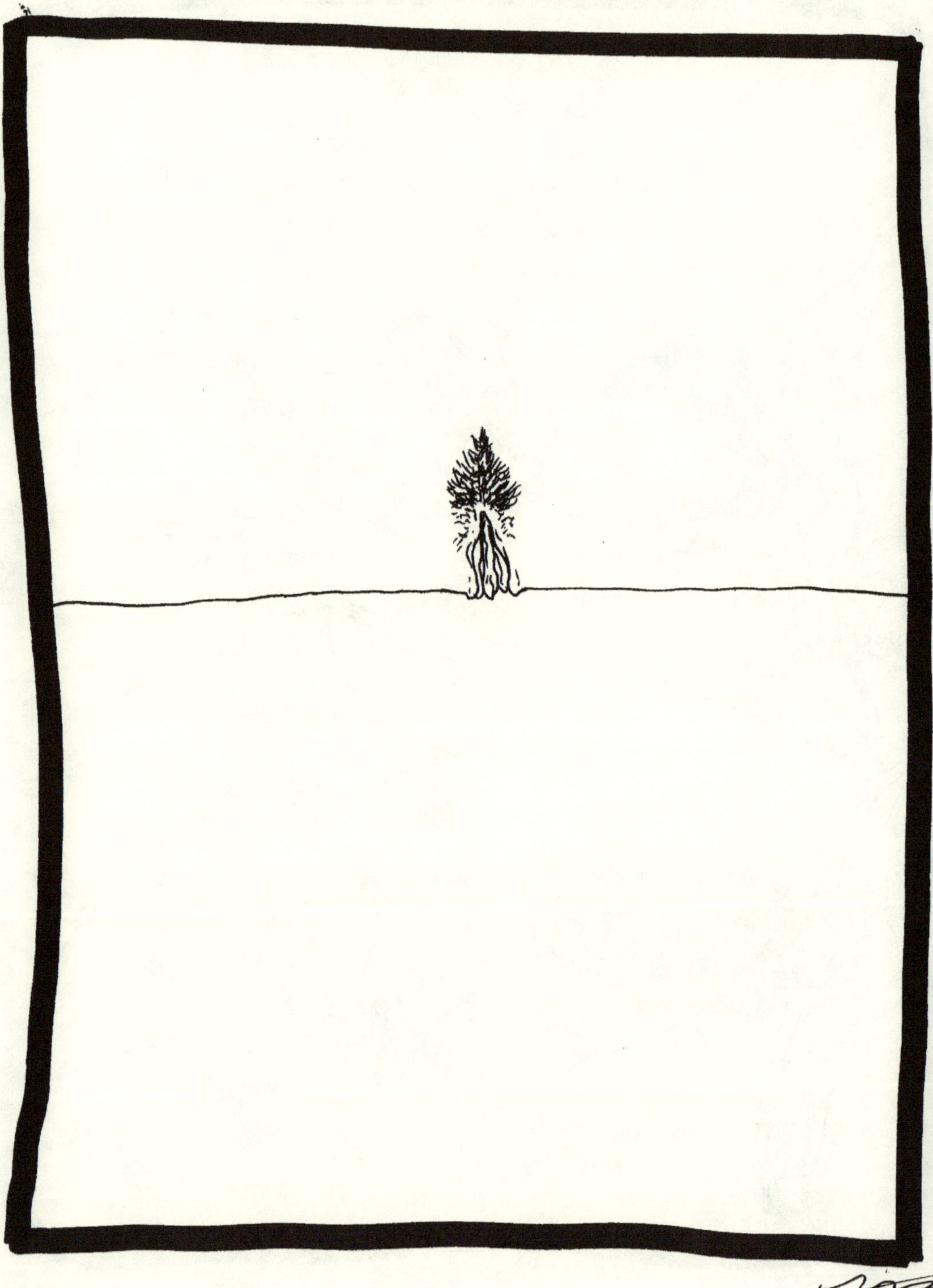

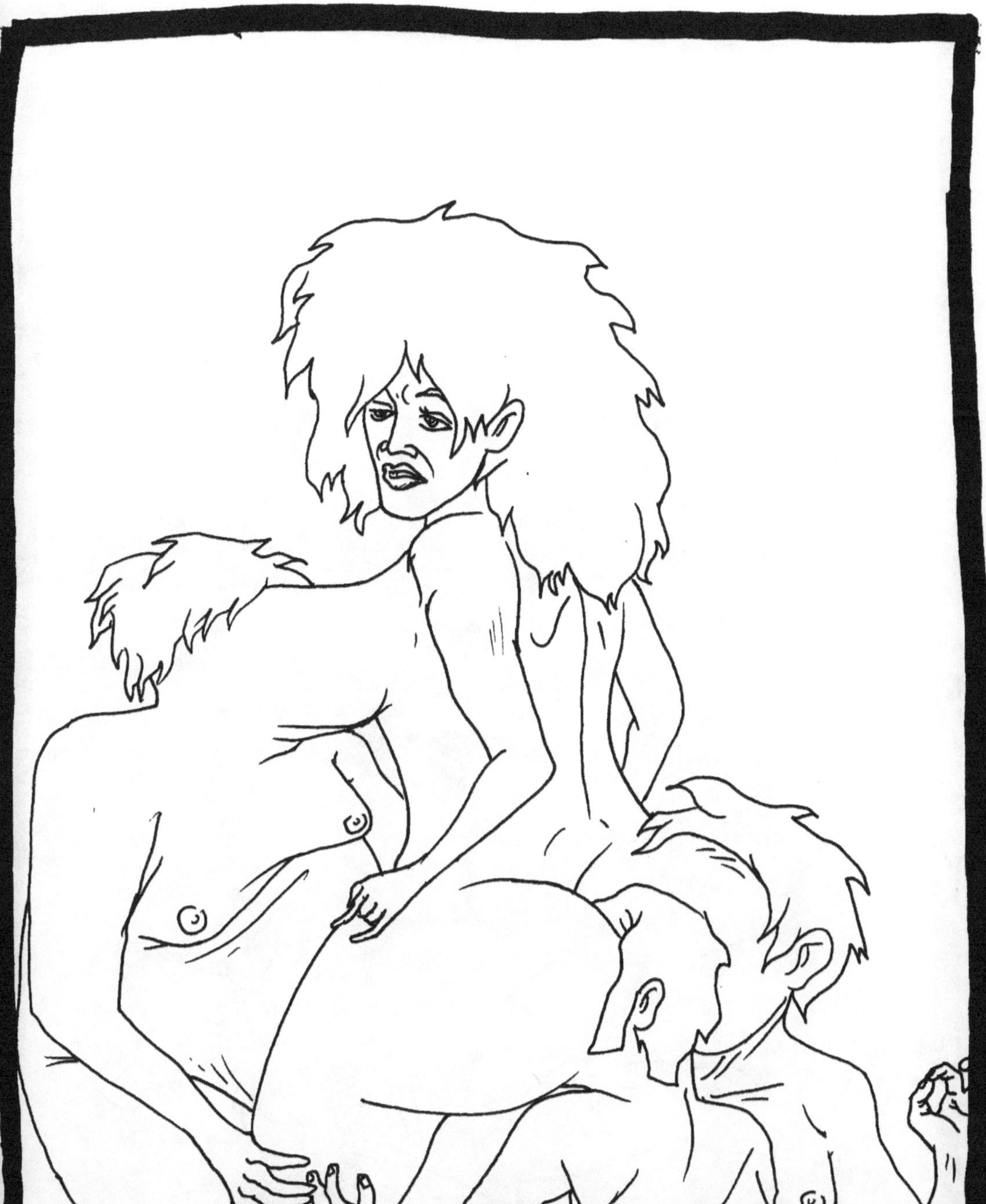

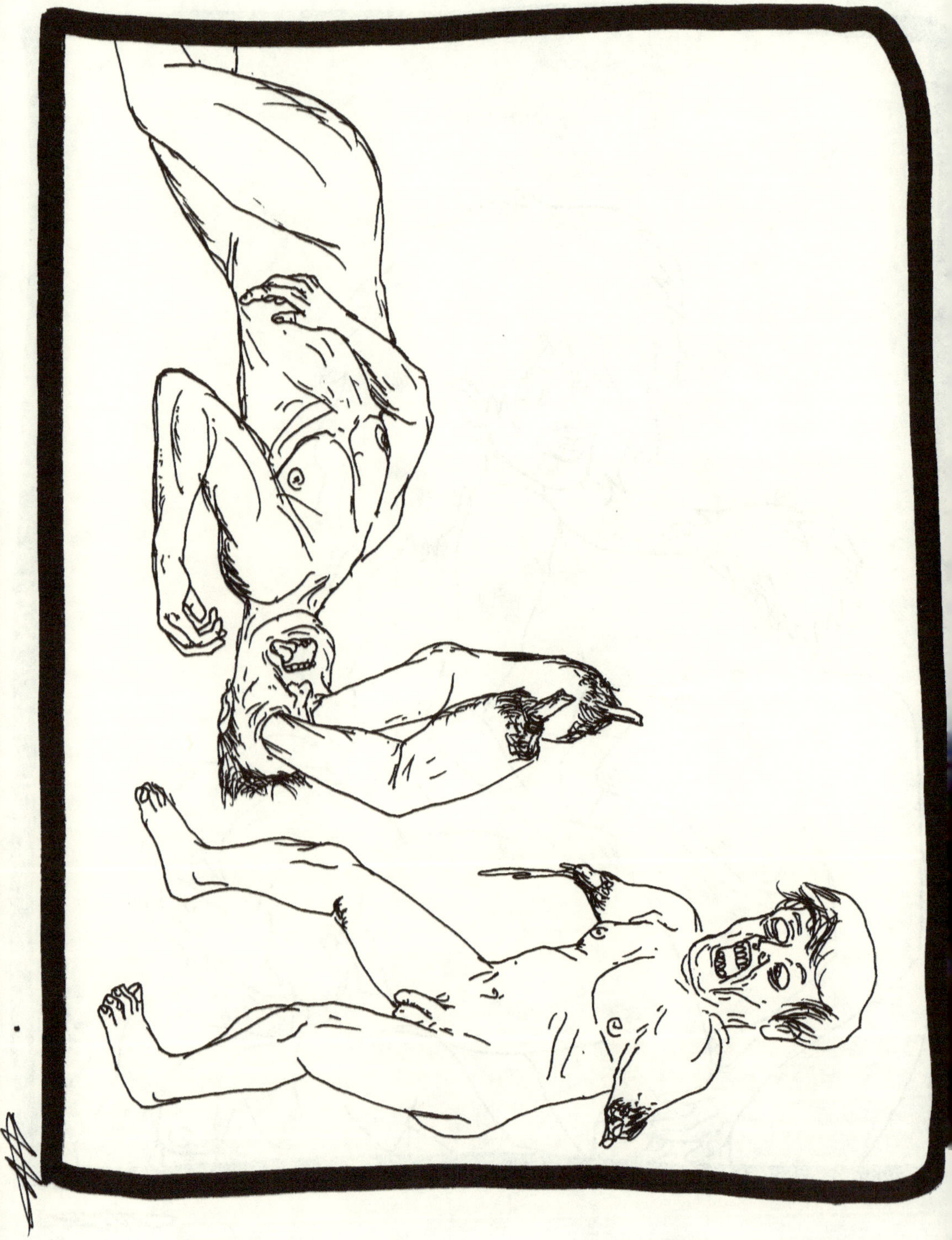

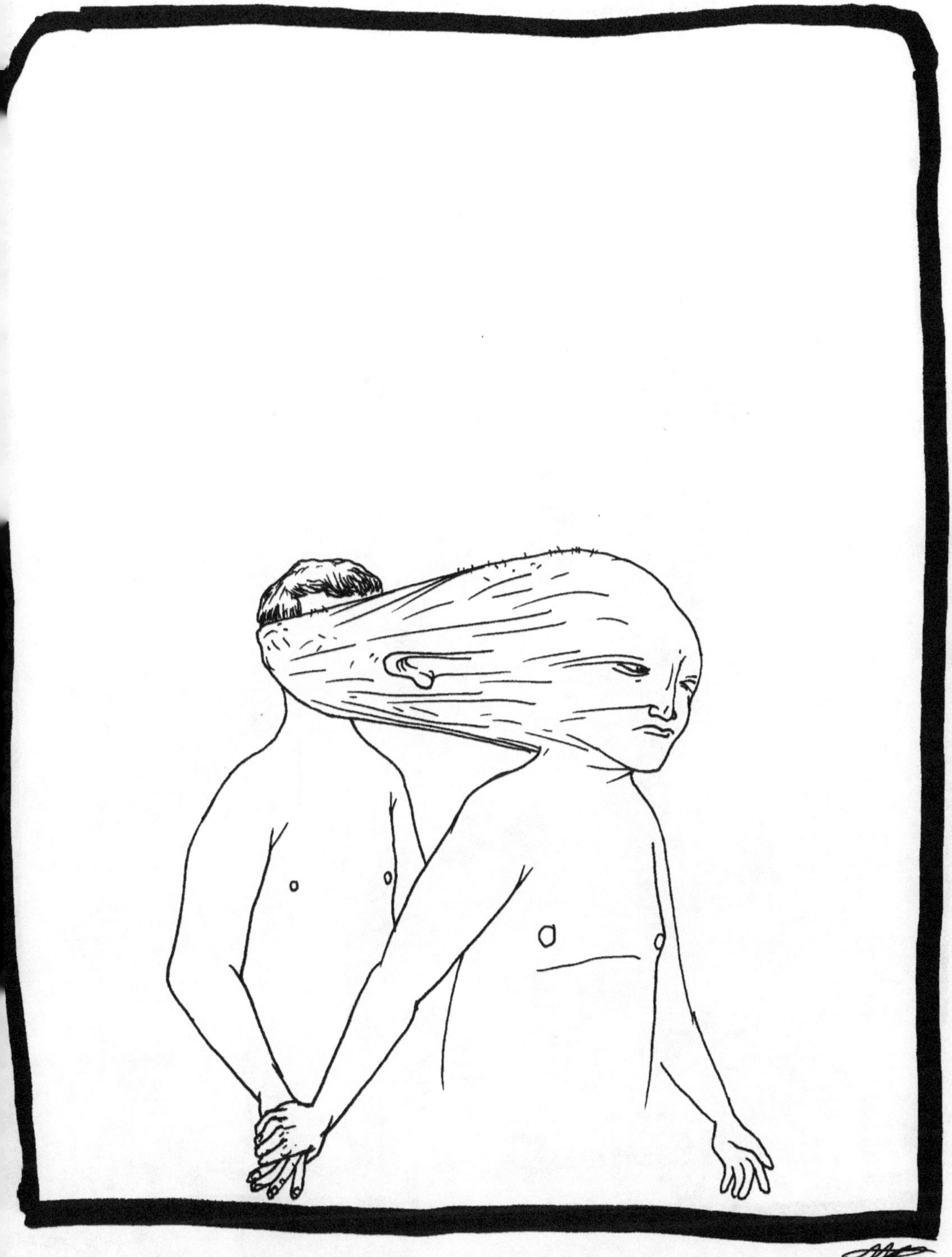

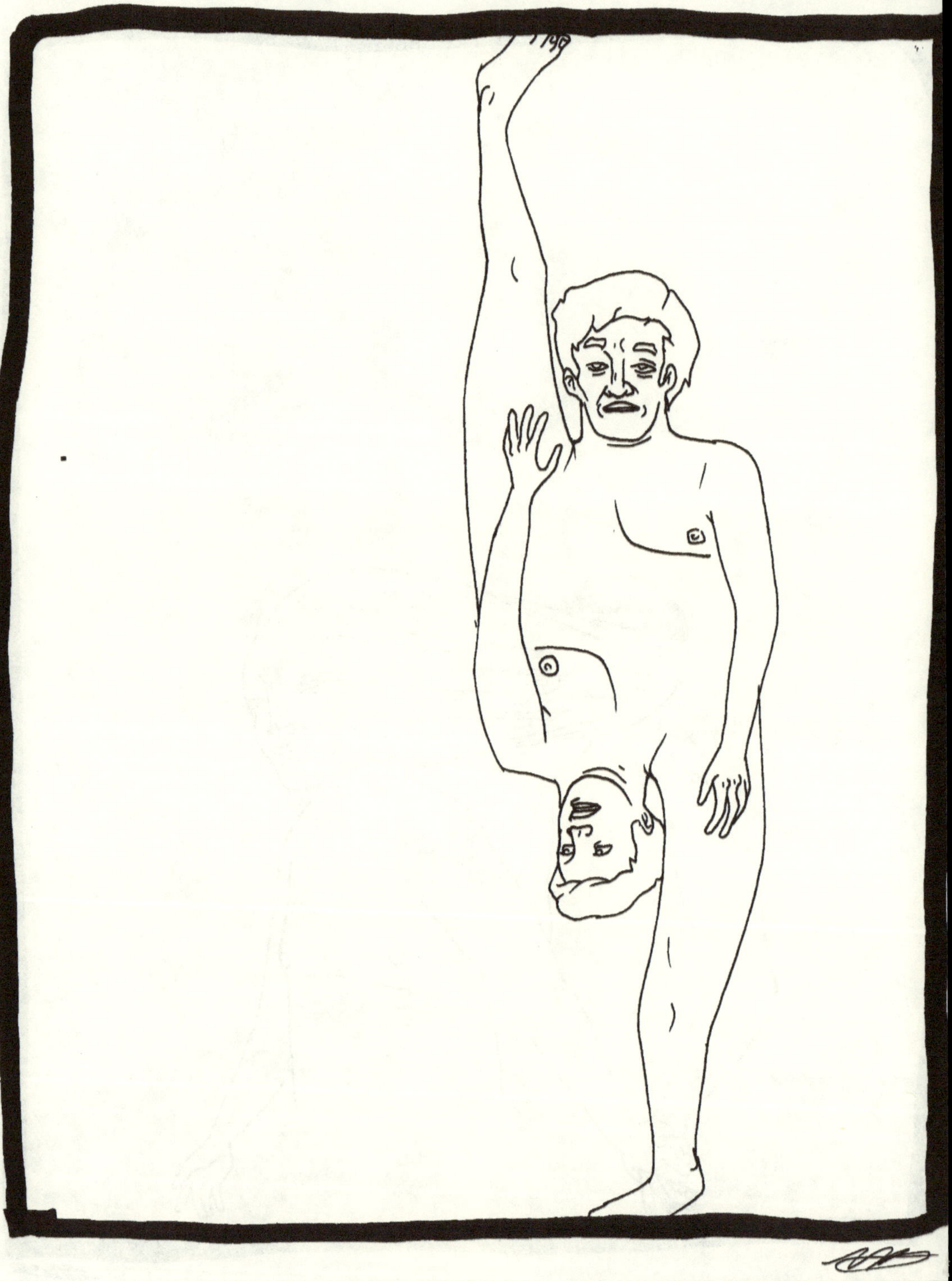

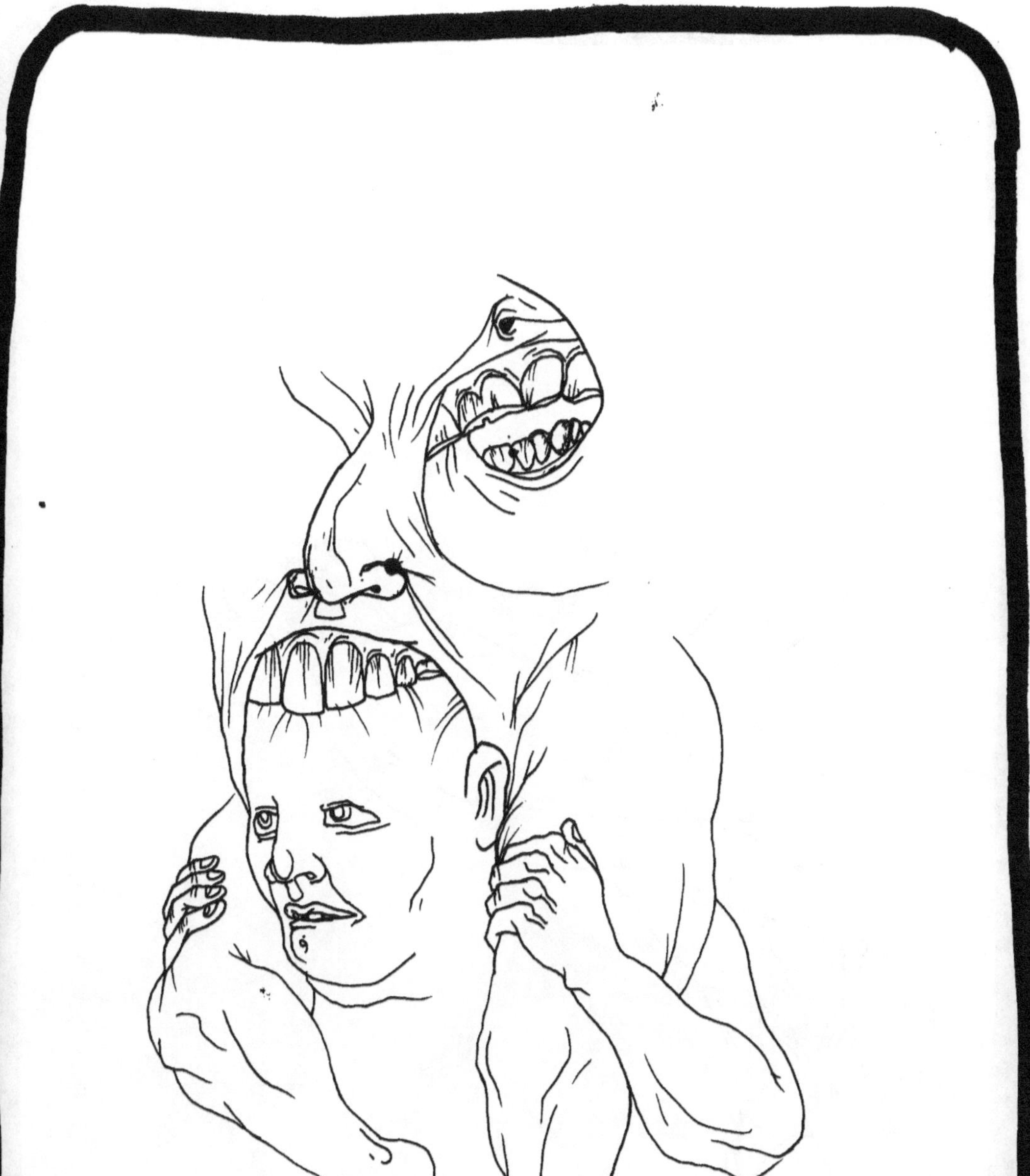

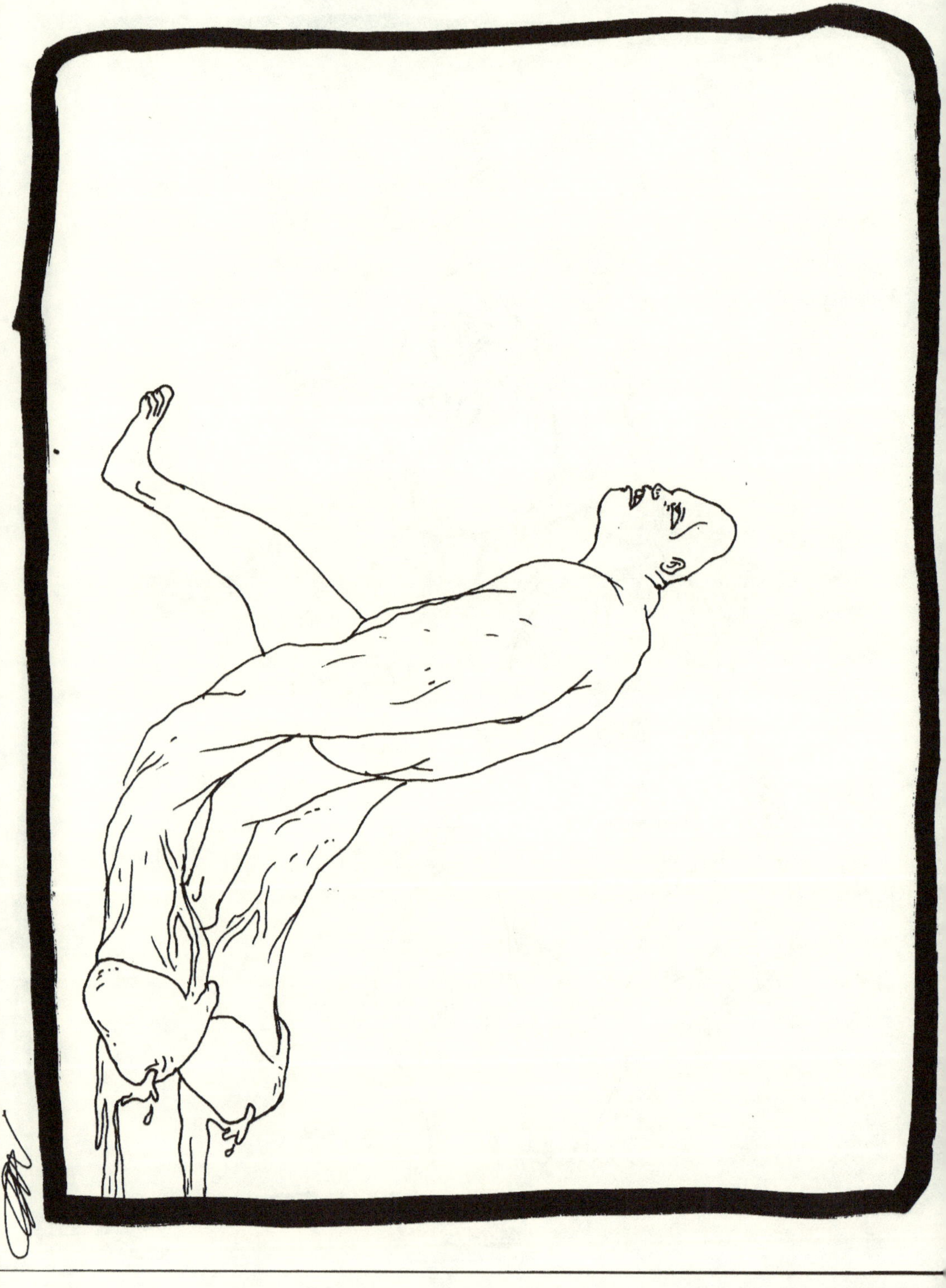

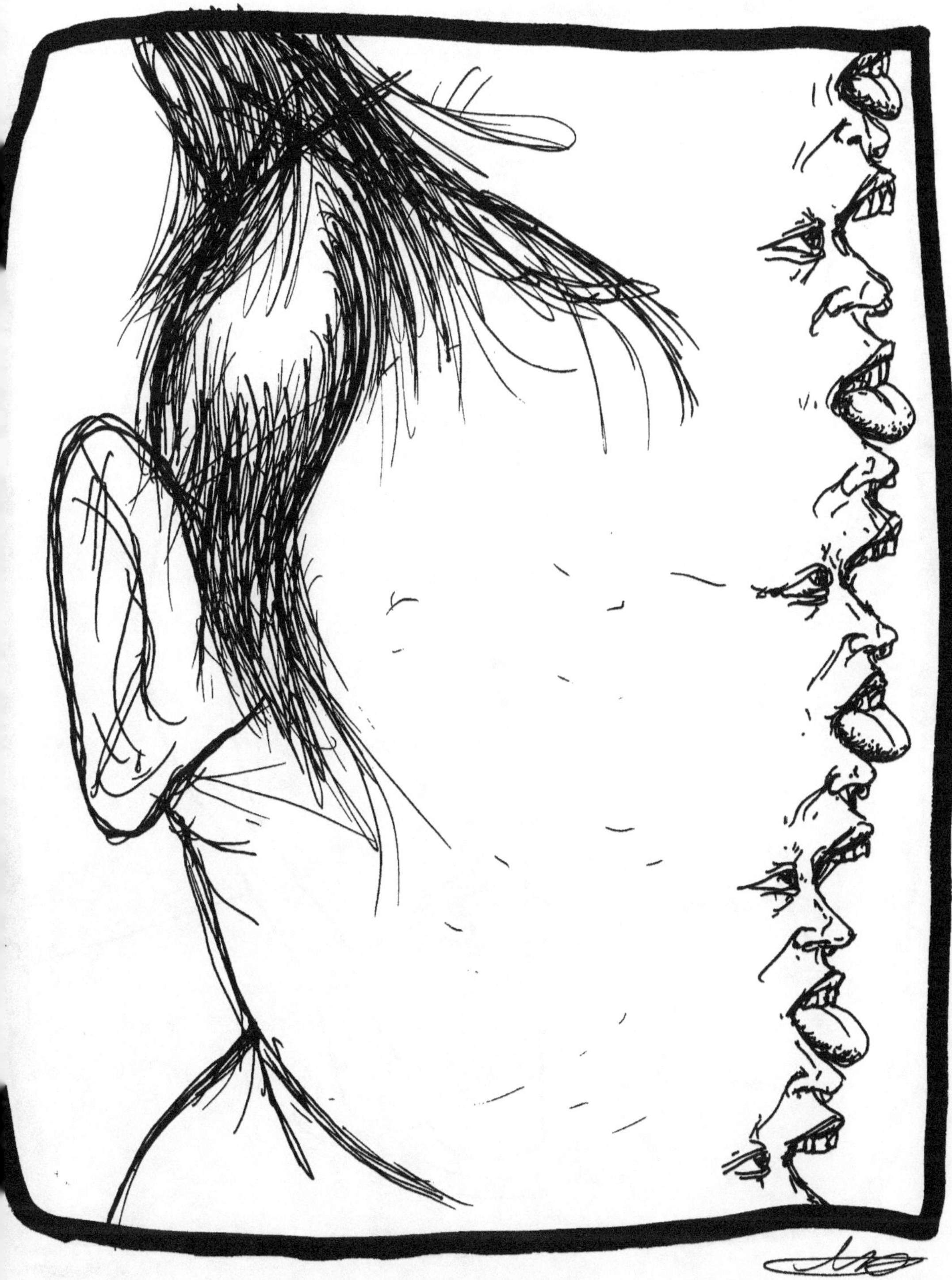

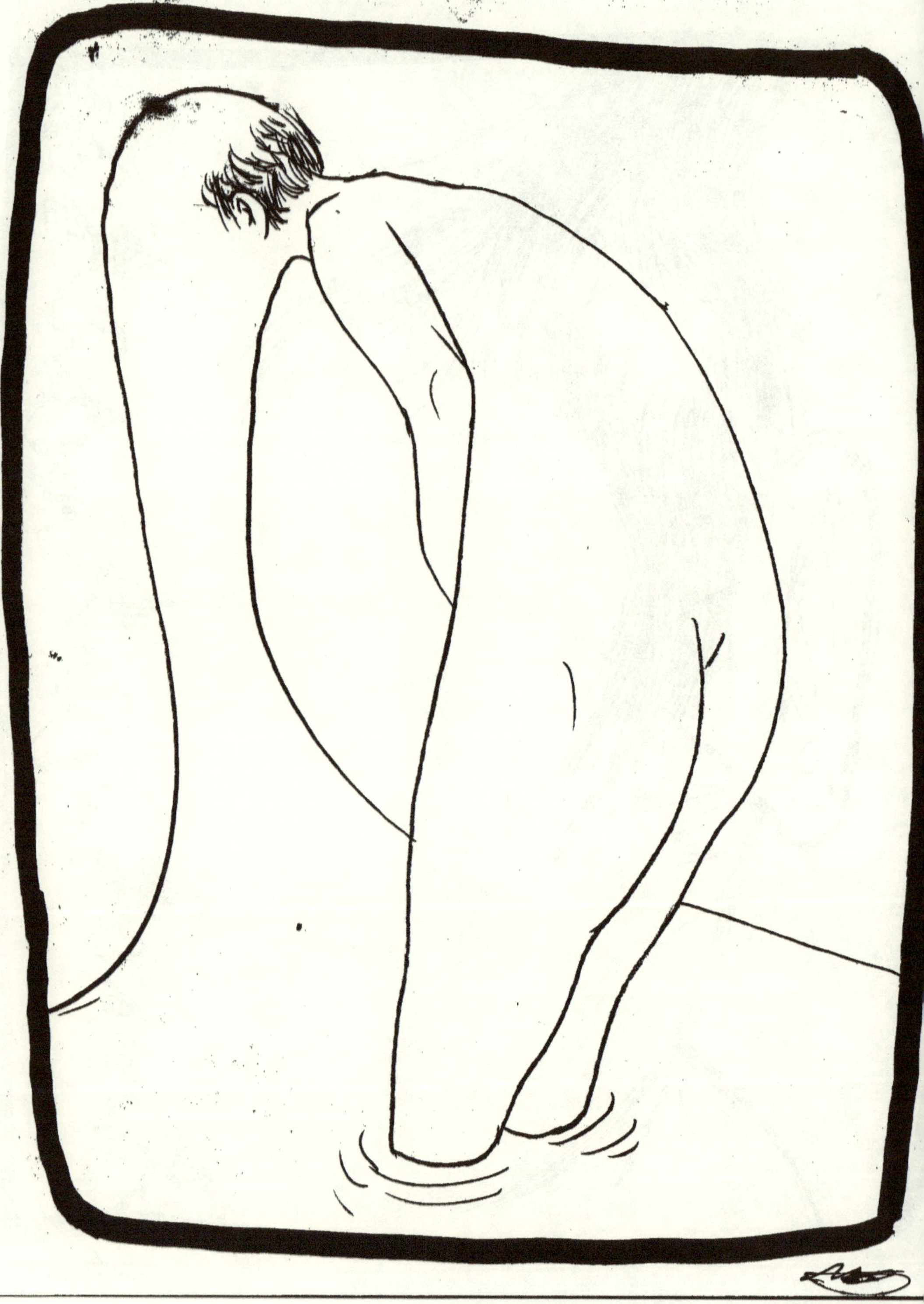

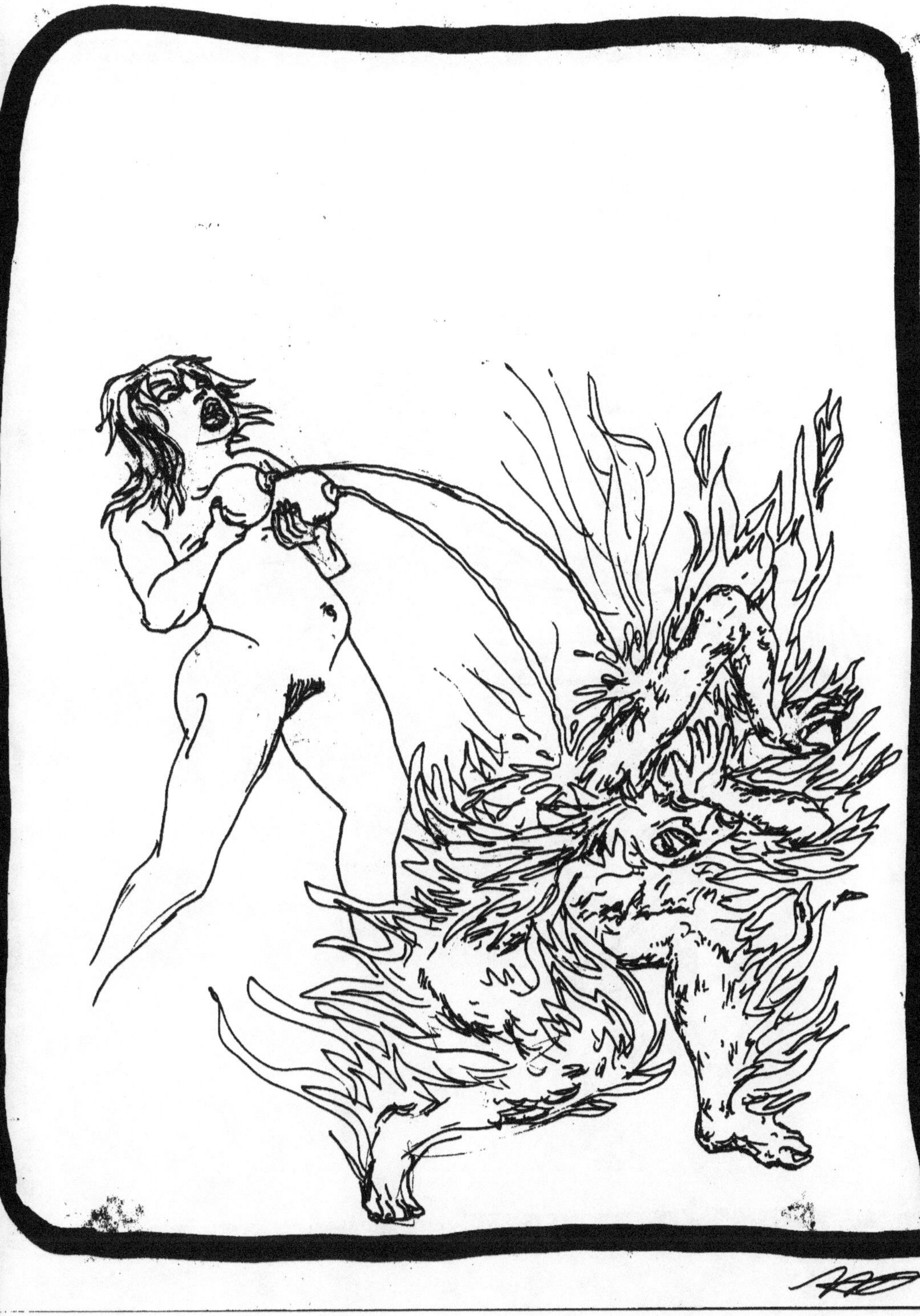

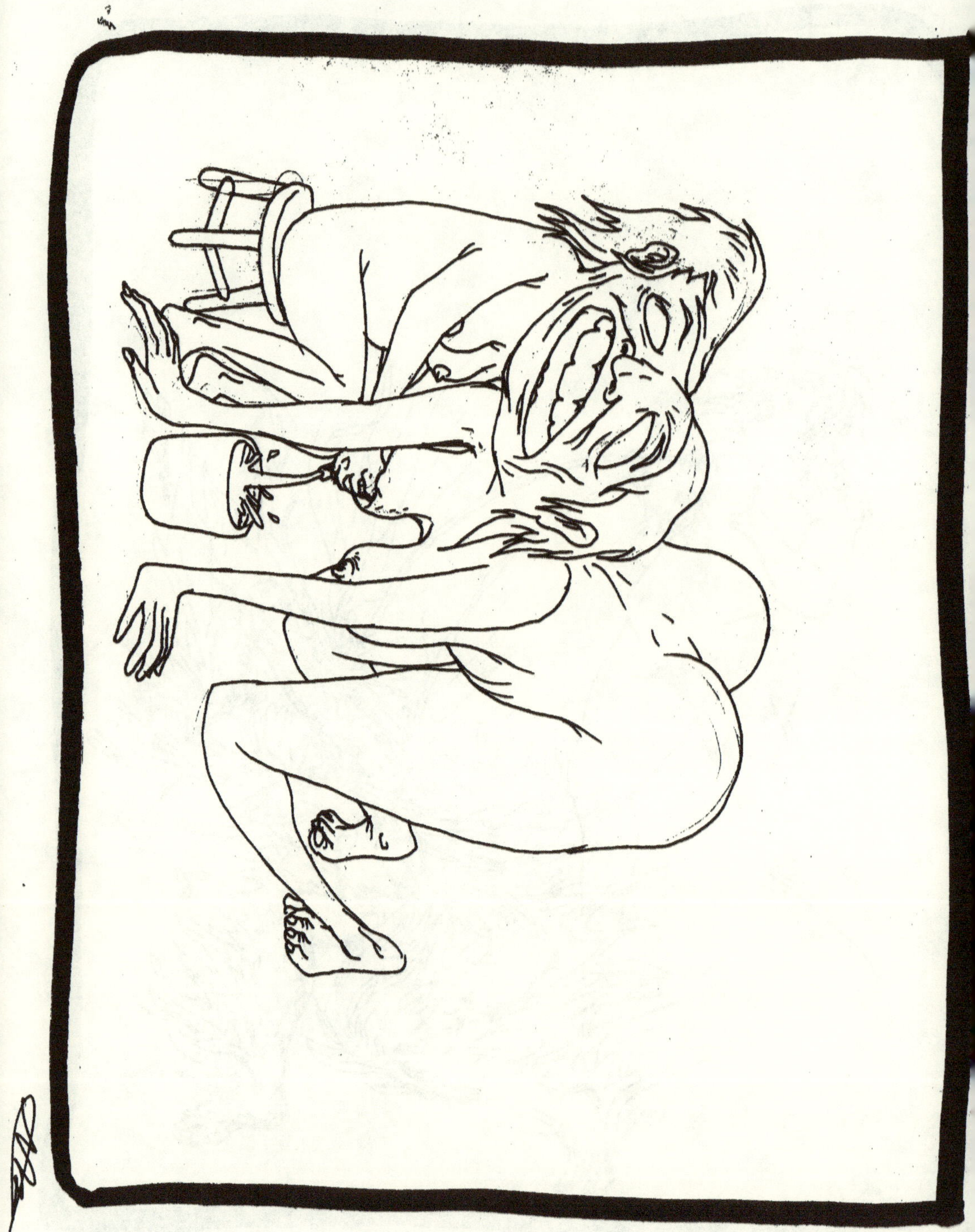

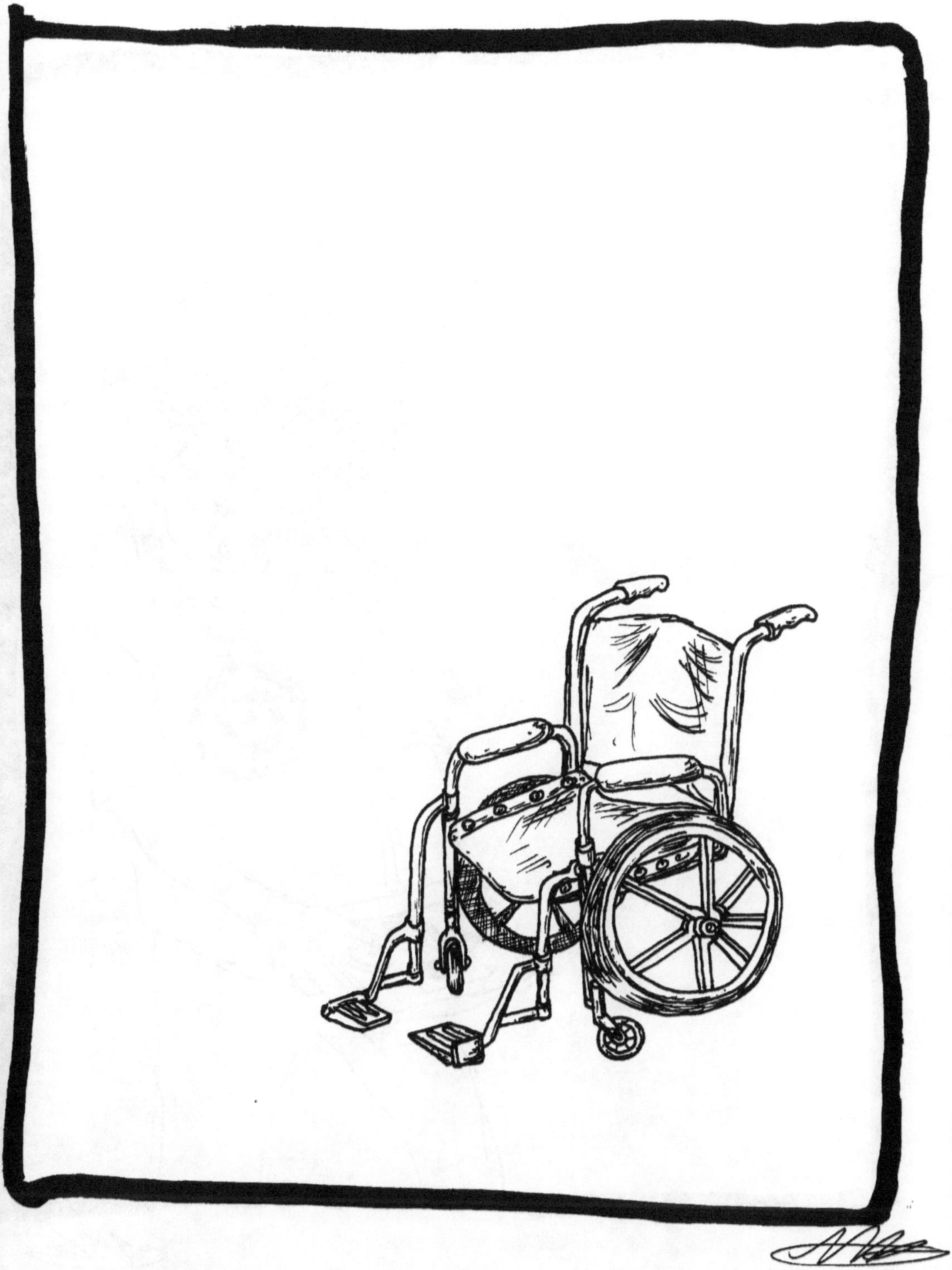

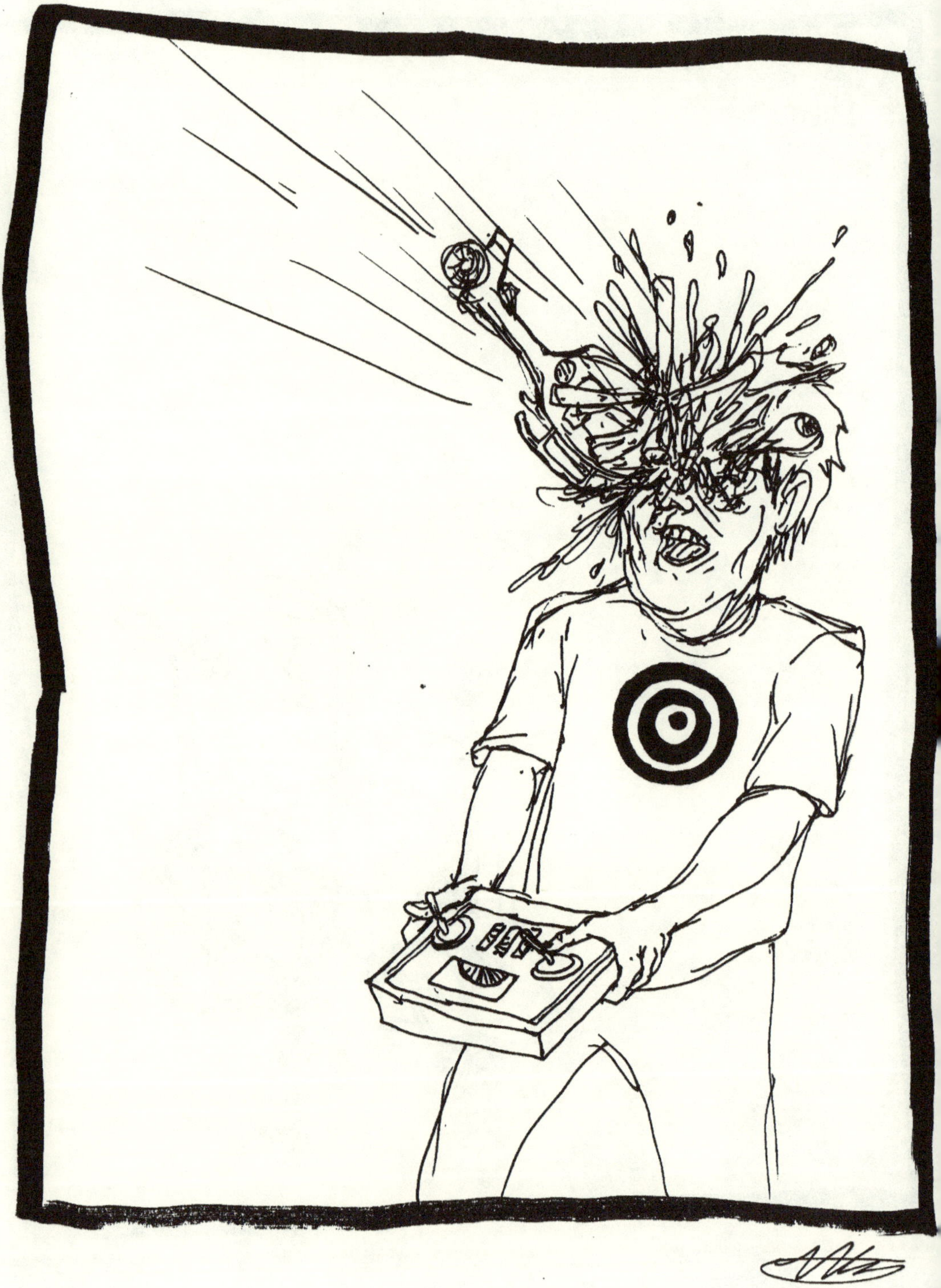

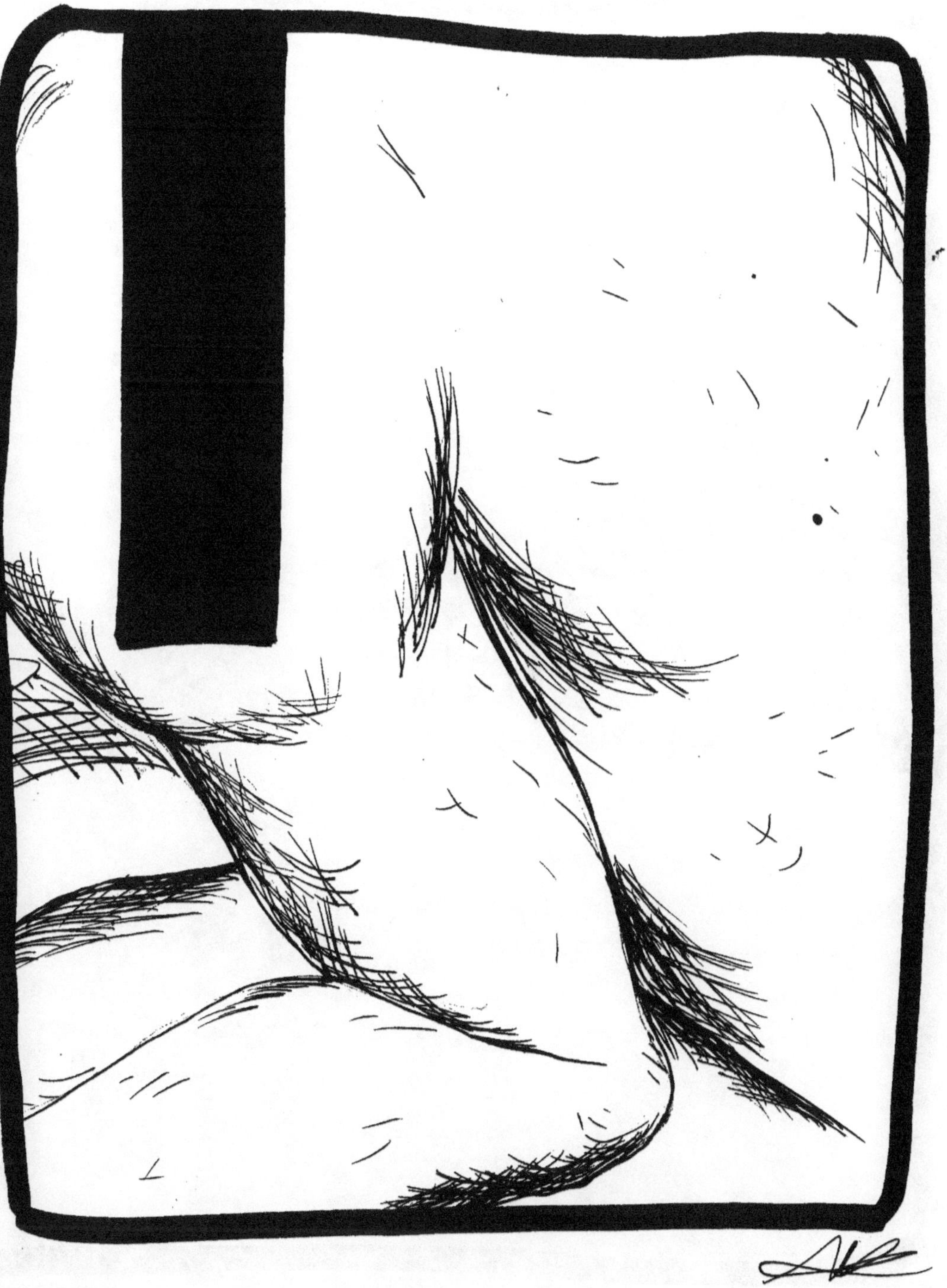

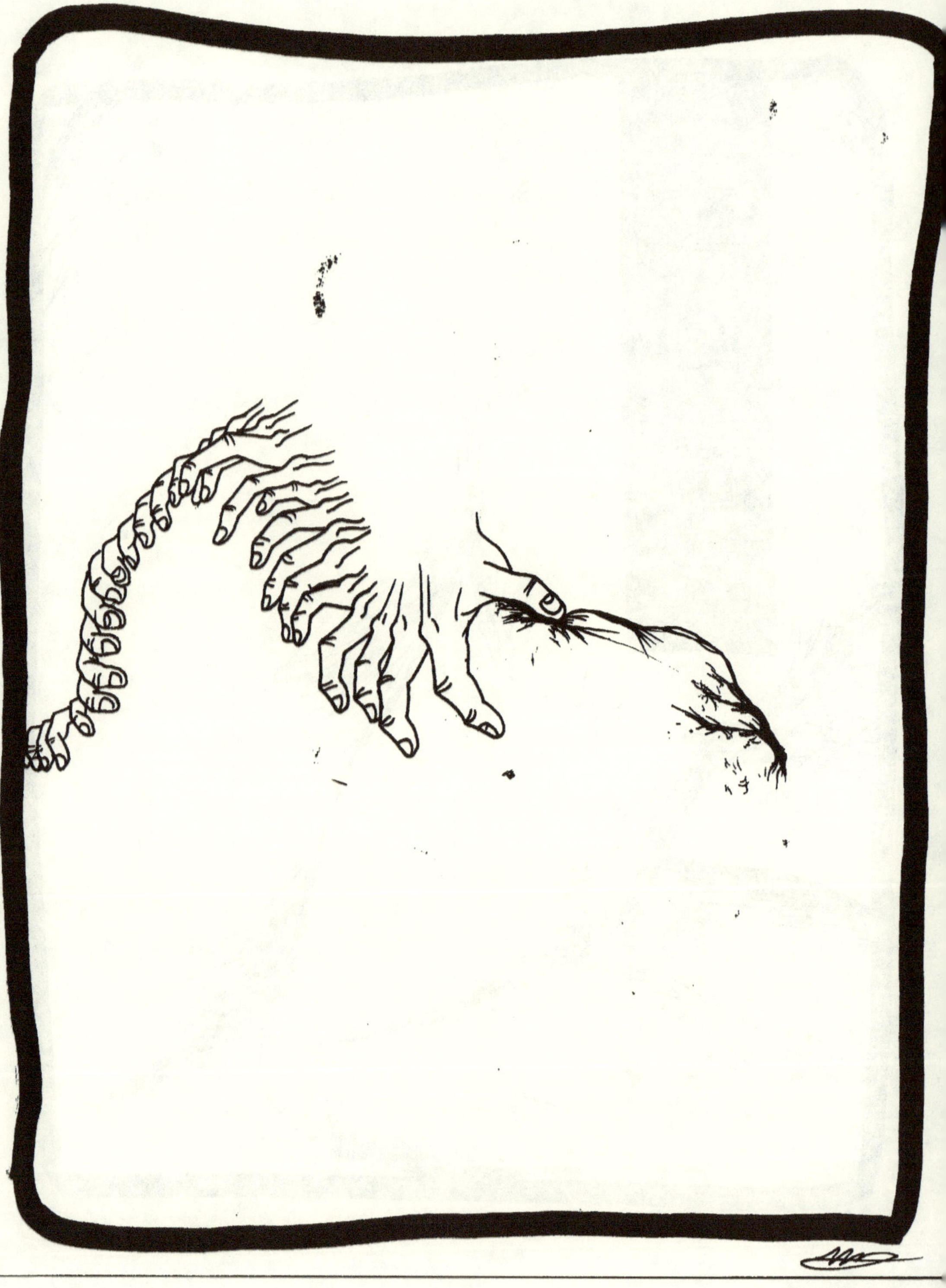

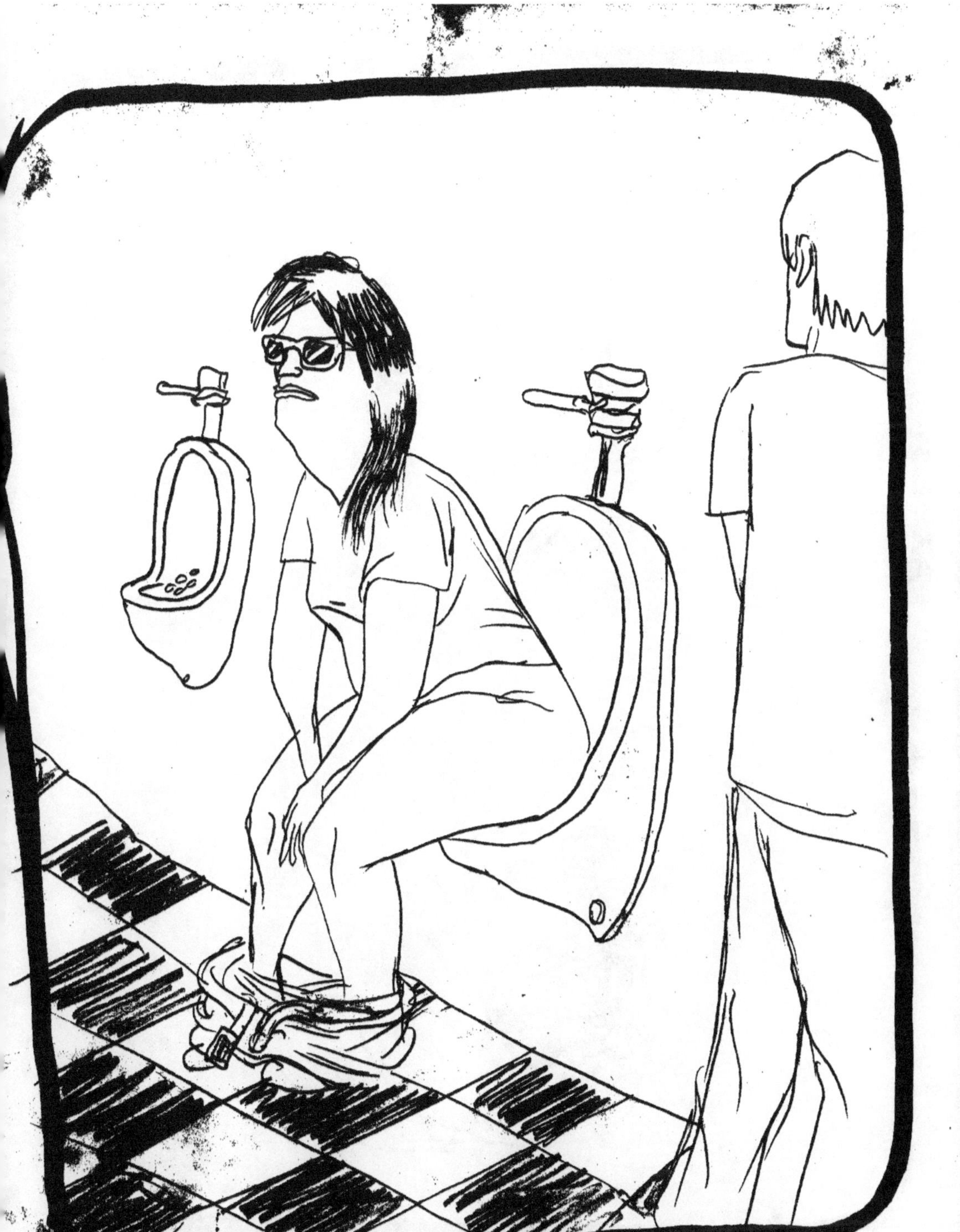

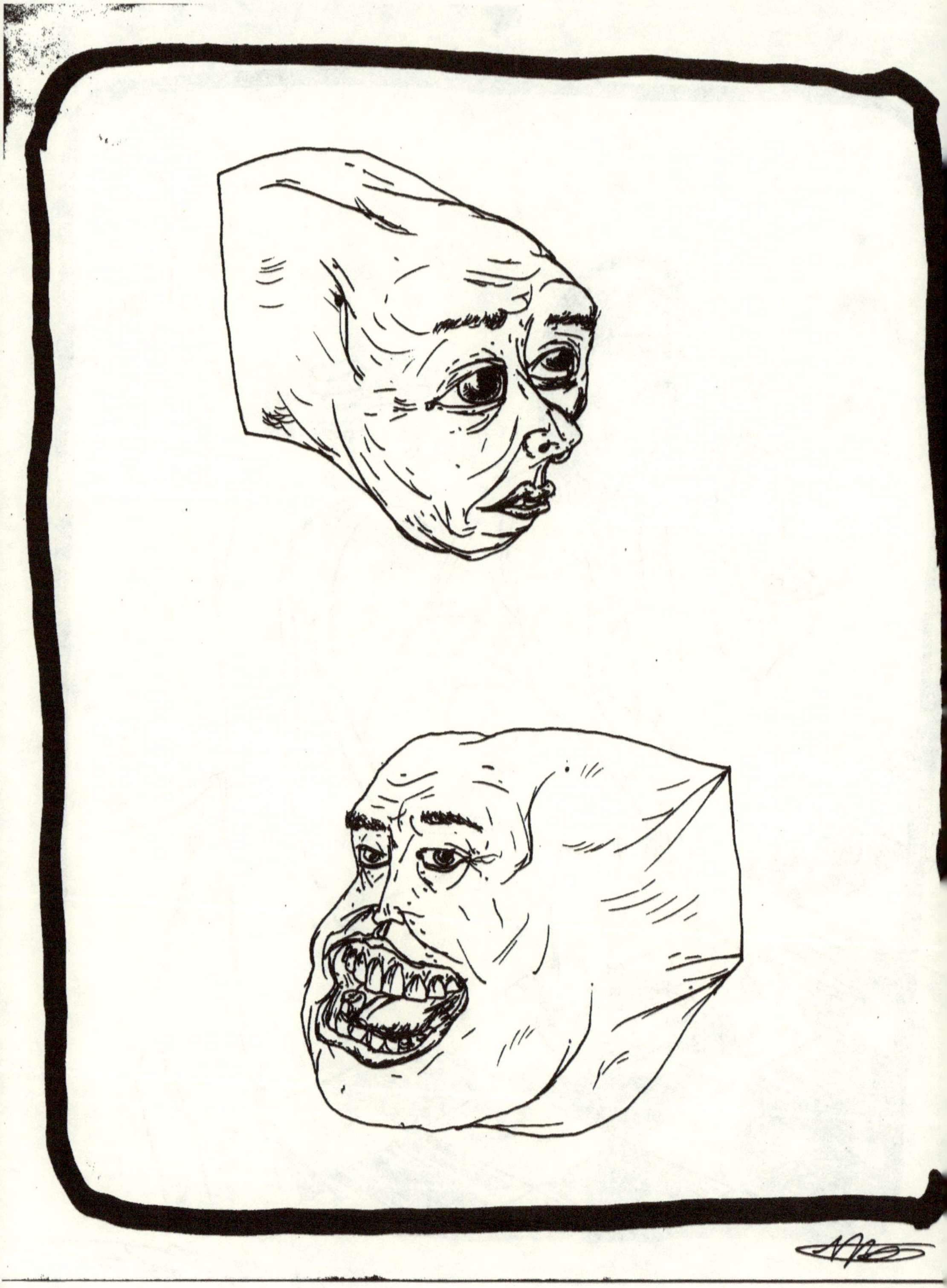

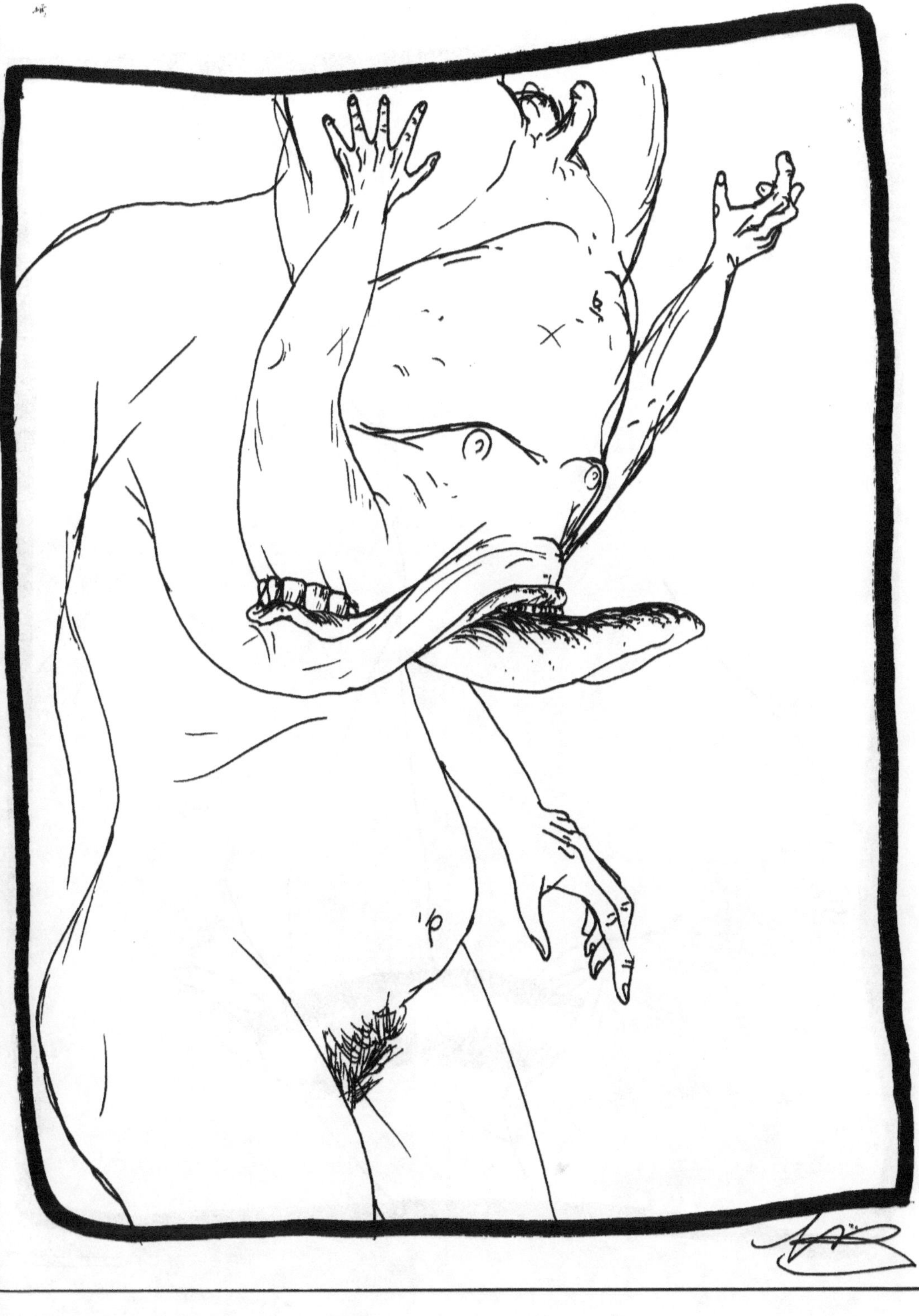

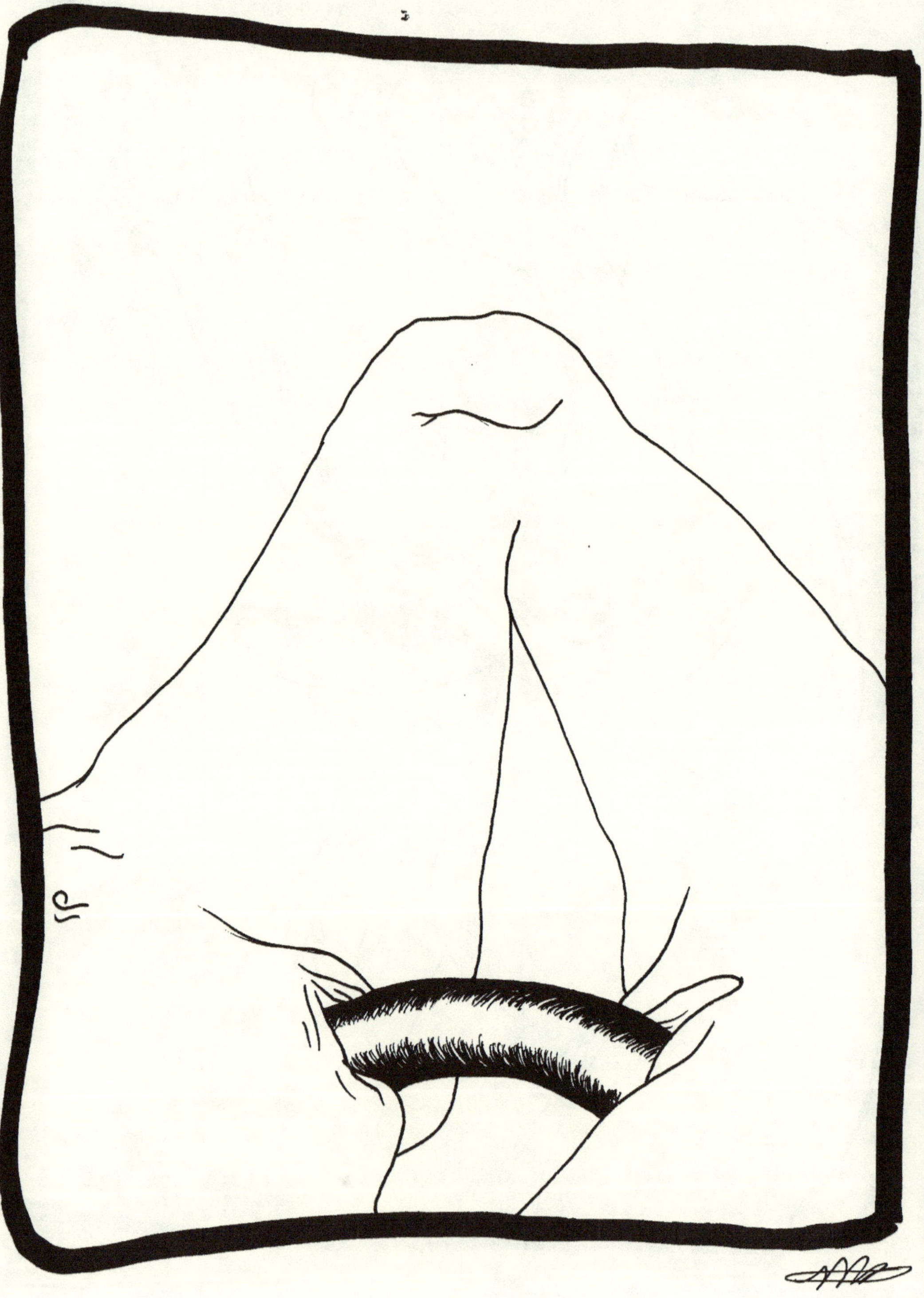

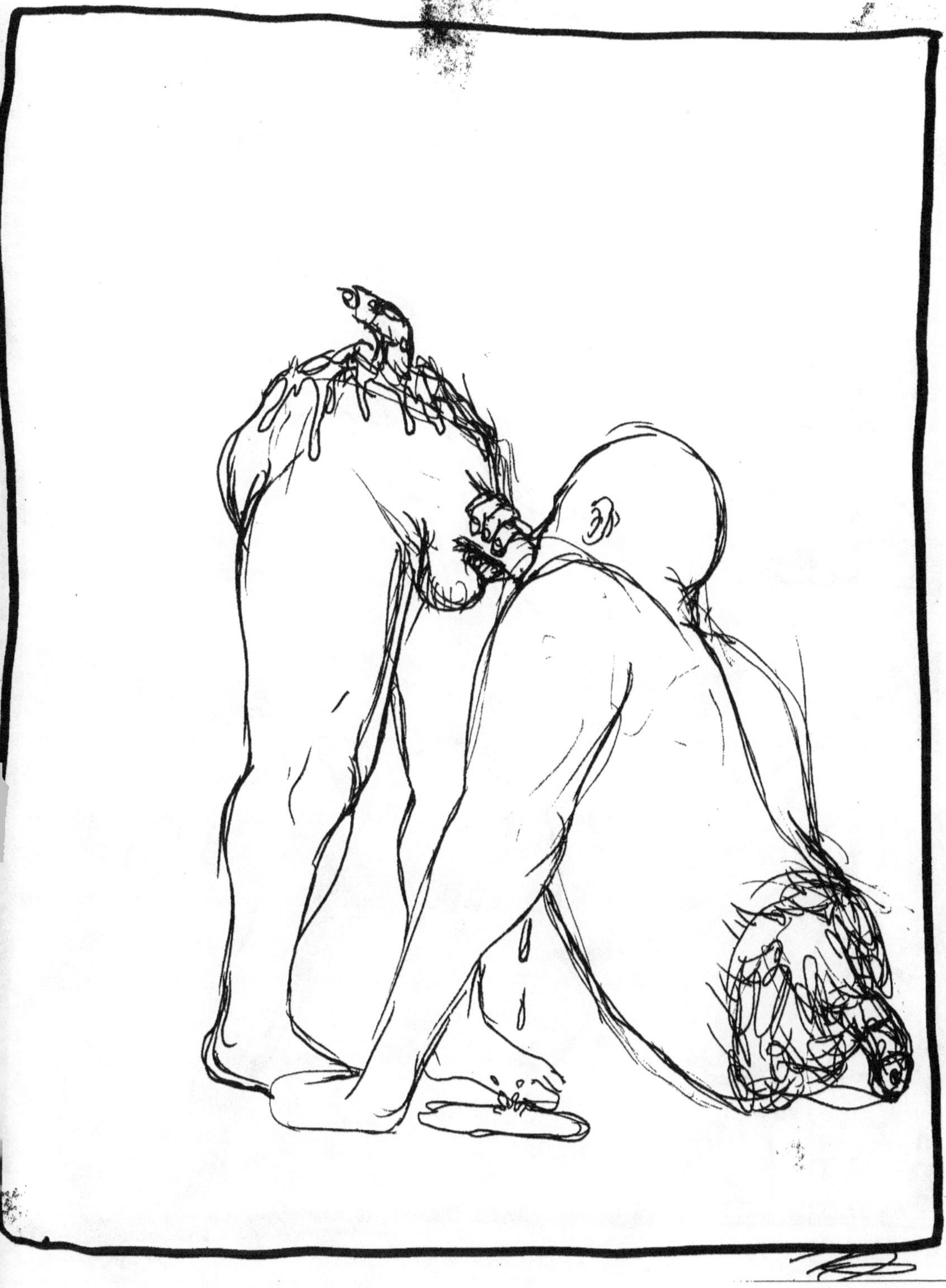

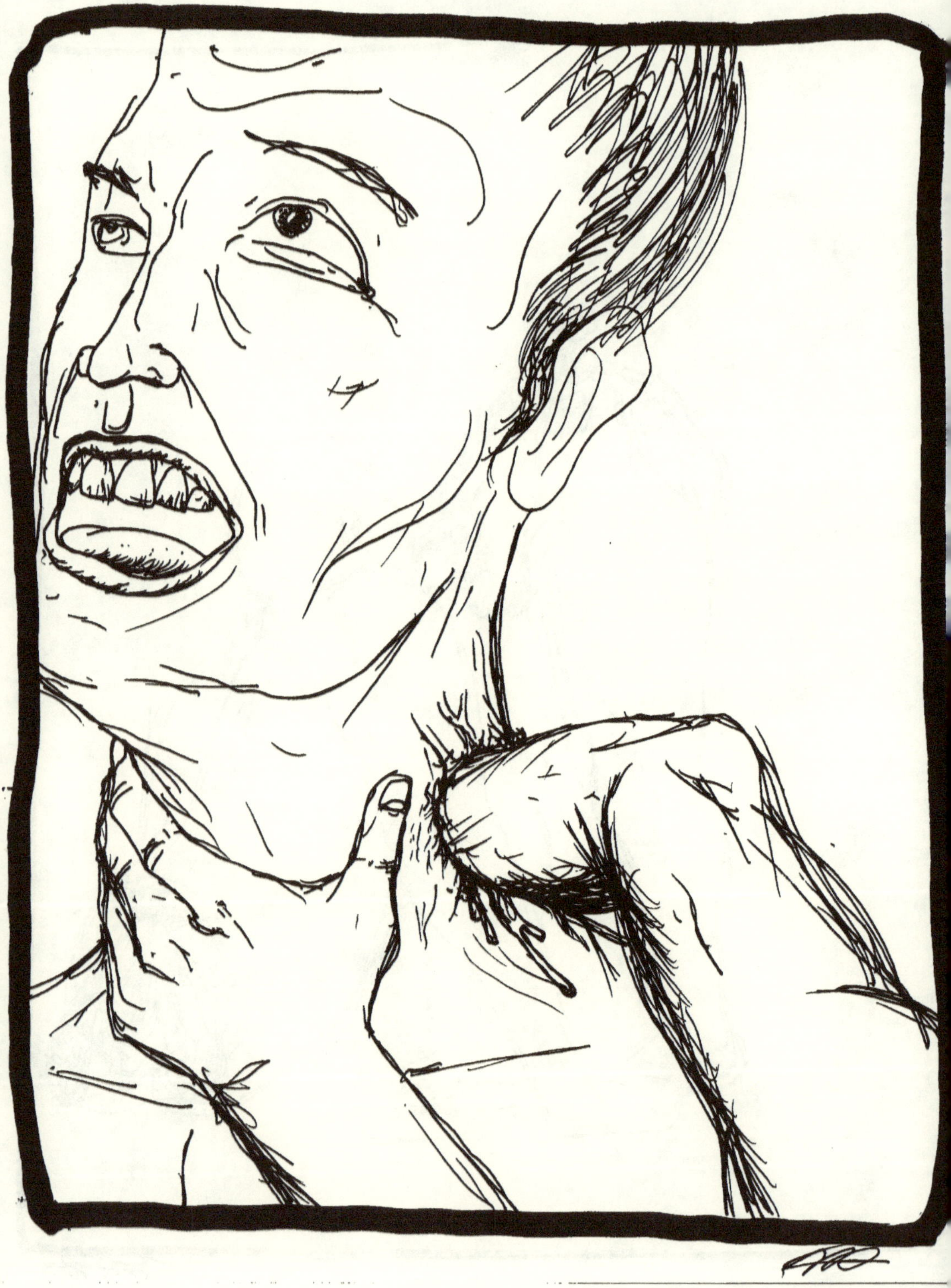

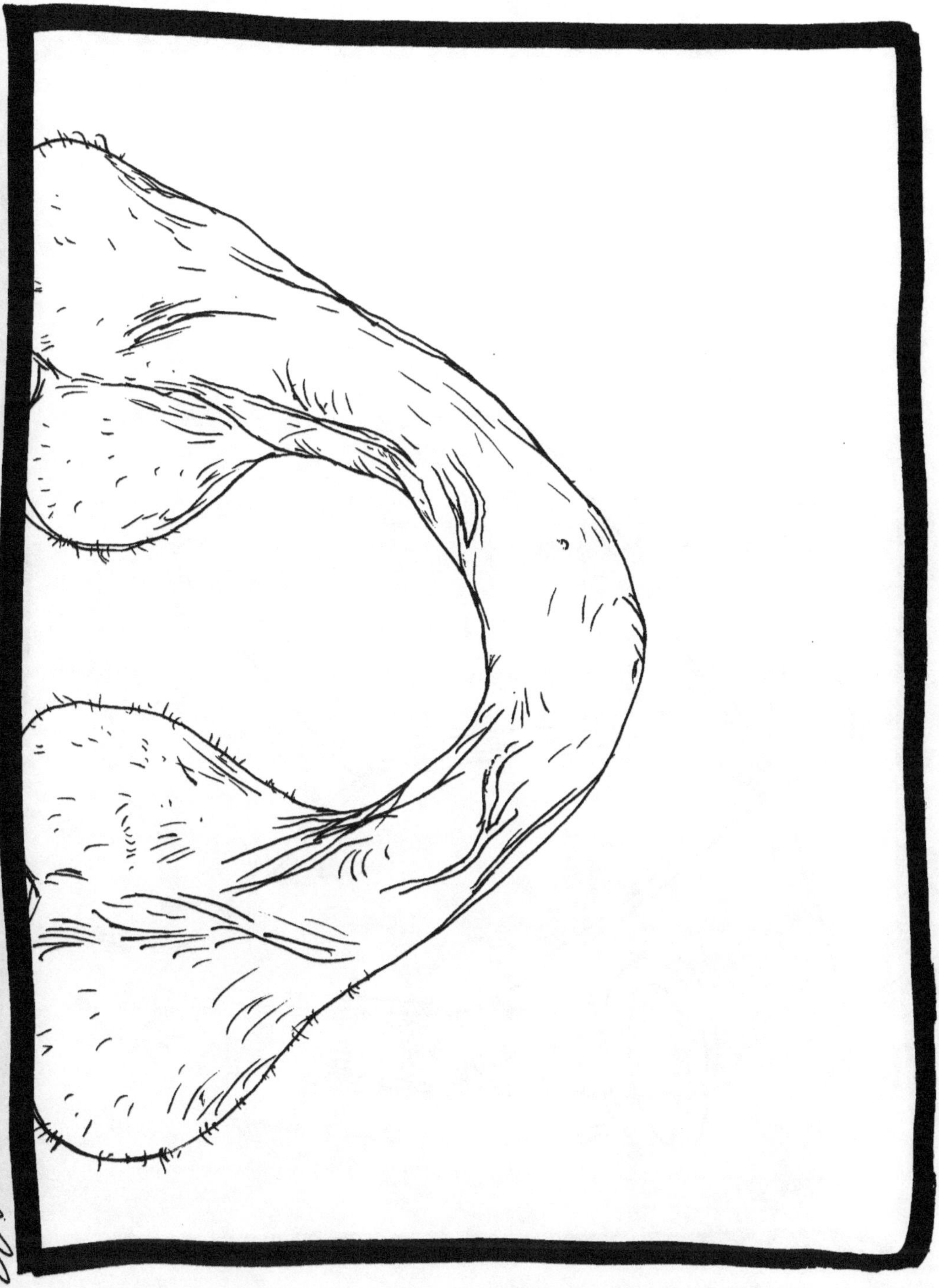

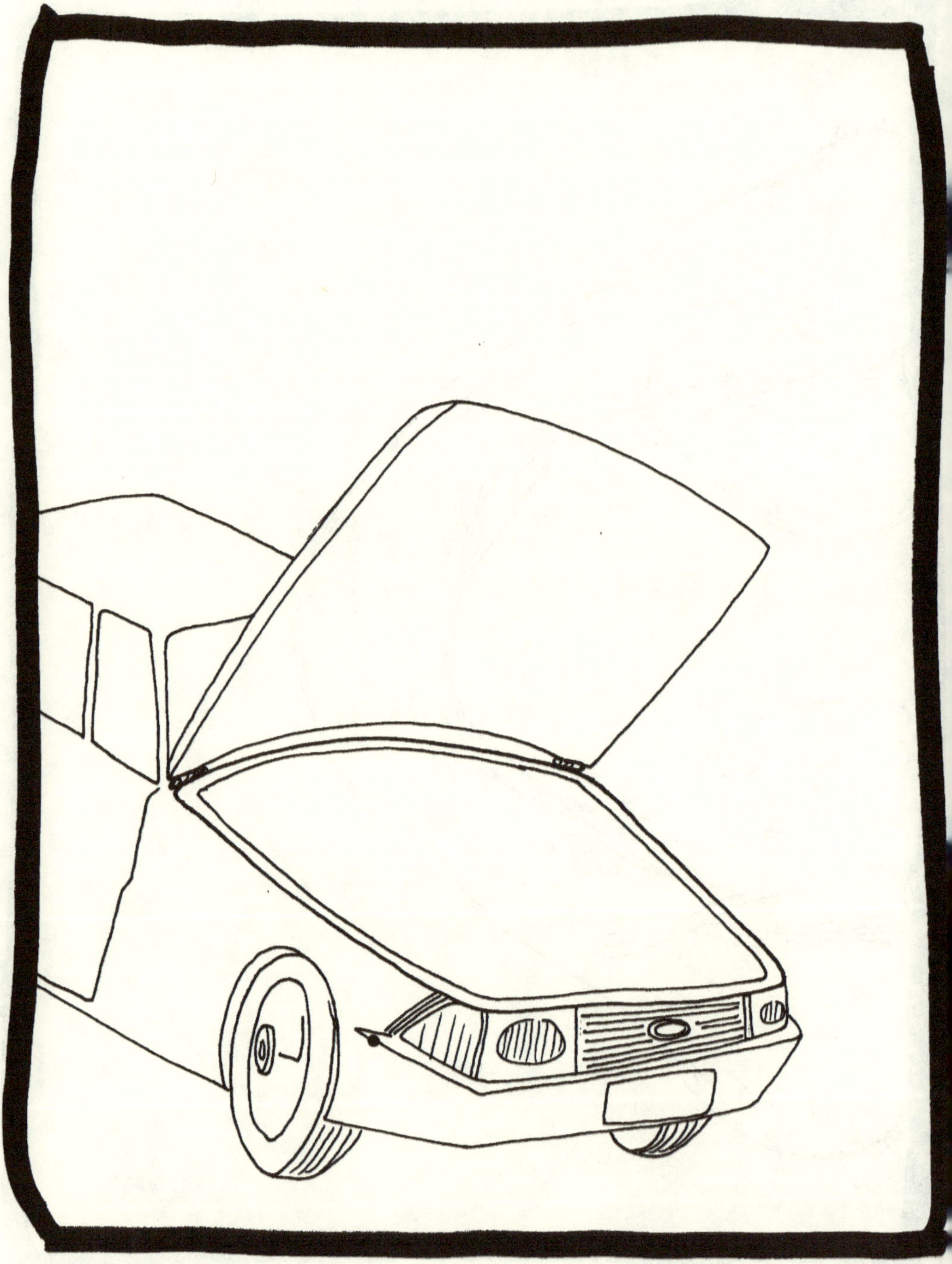

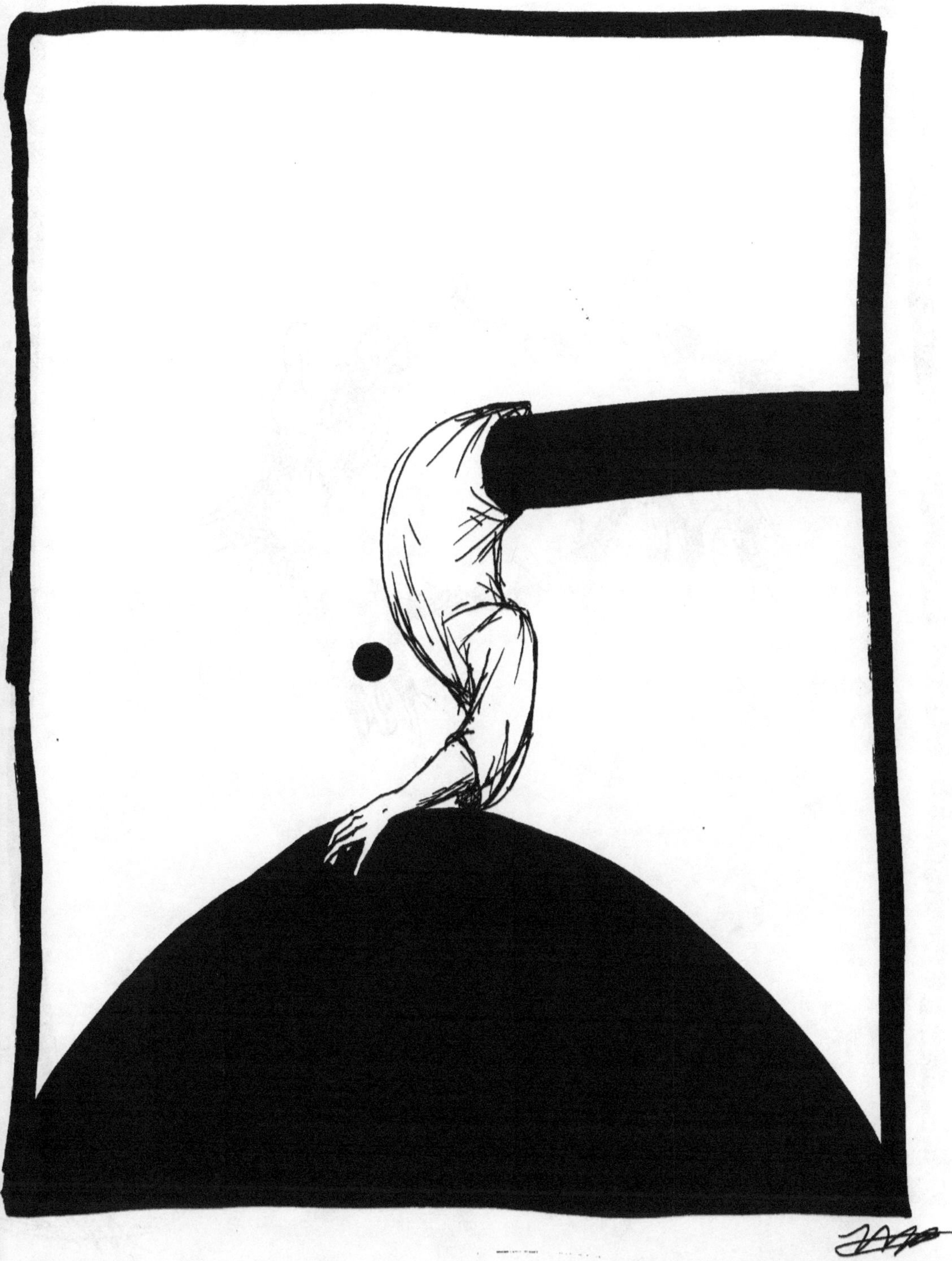

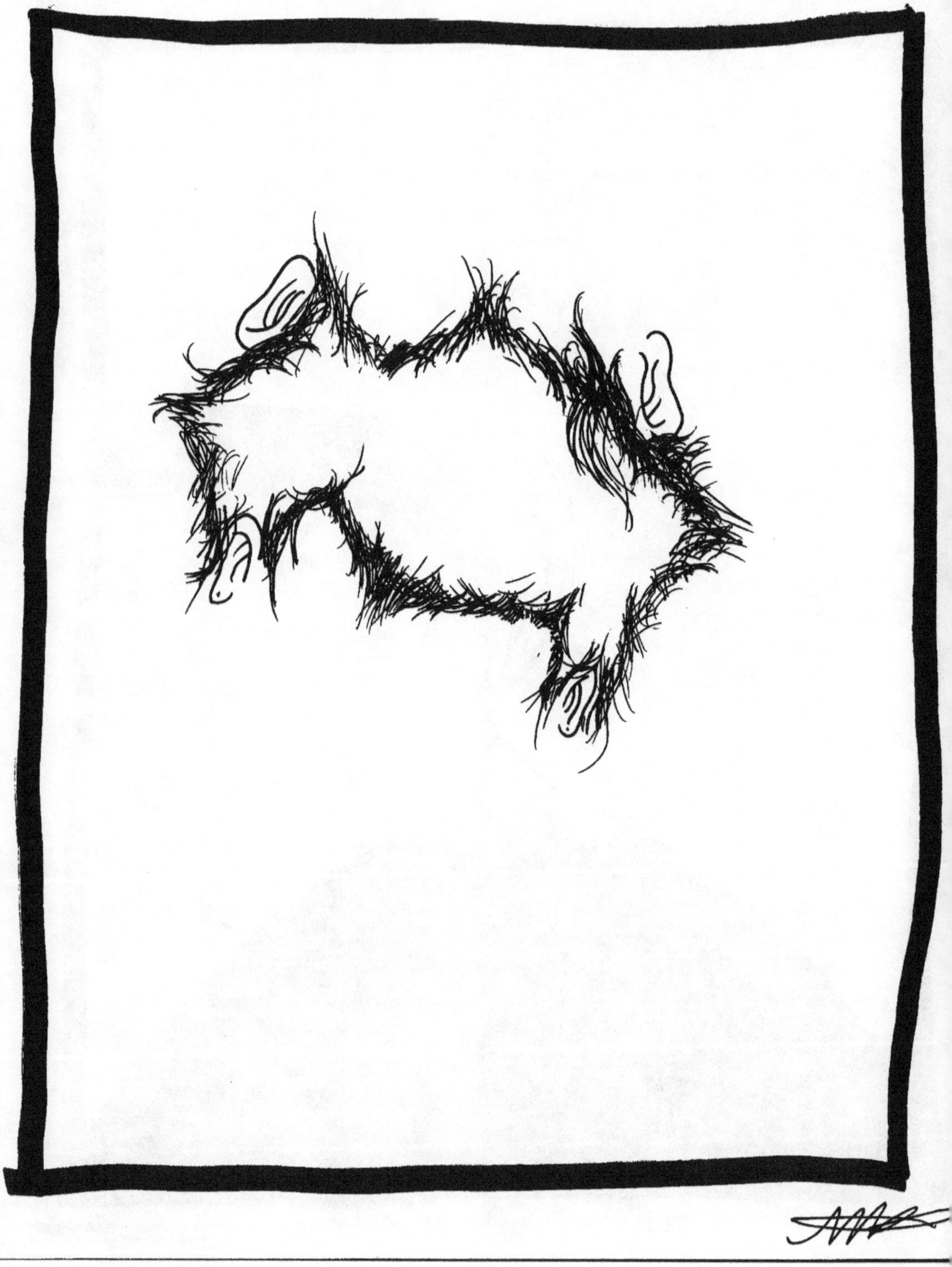

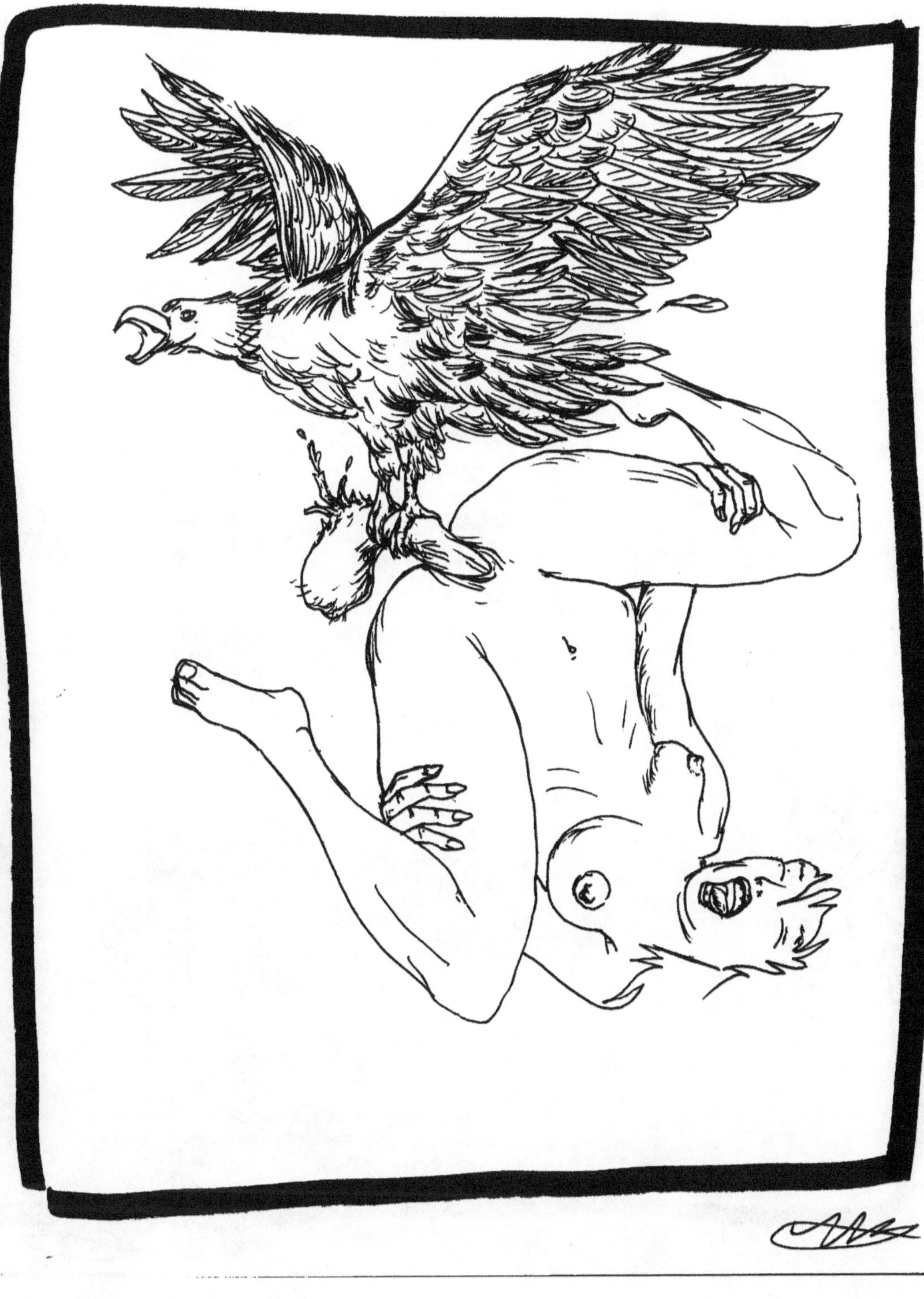

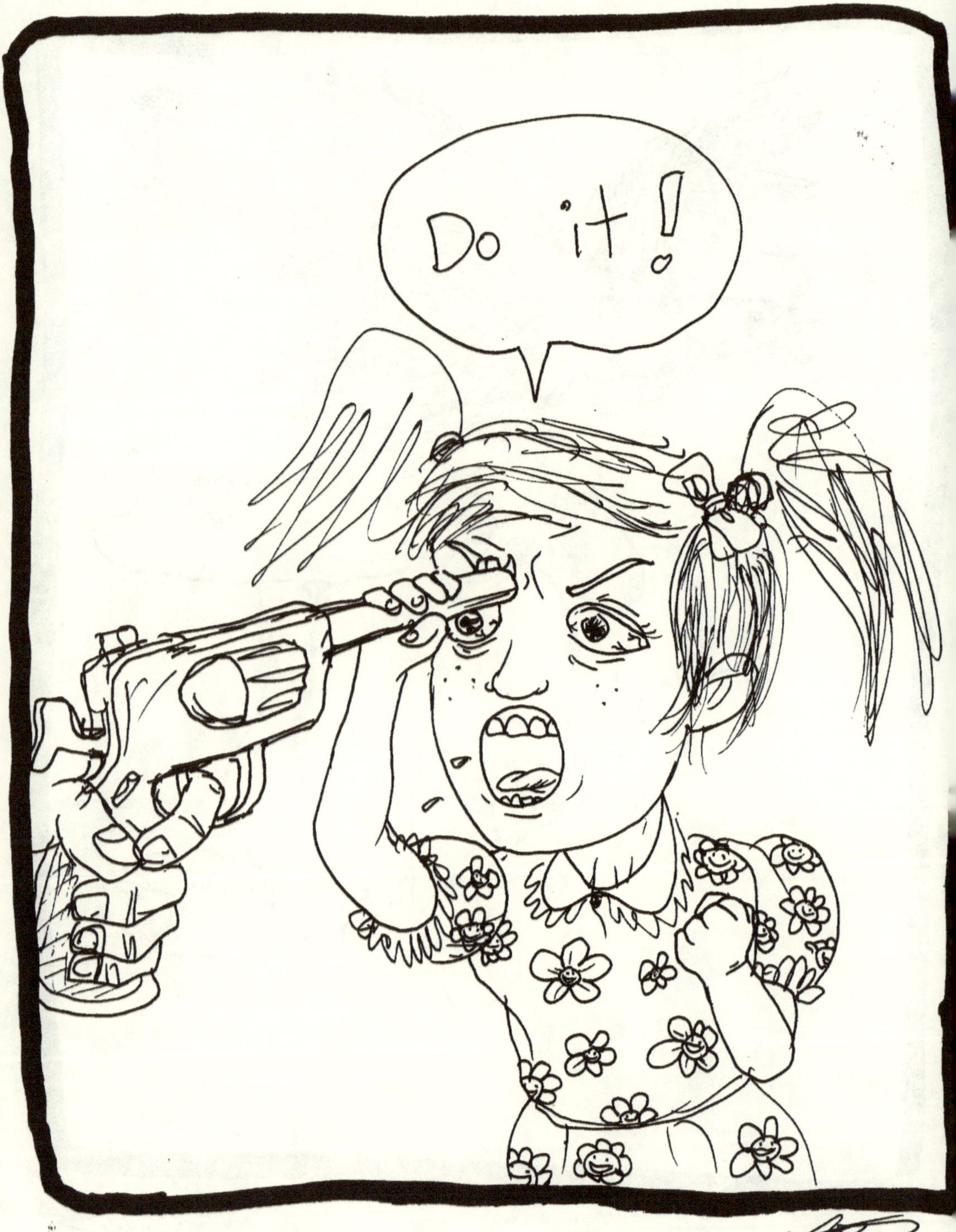
Do it!

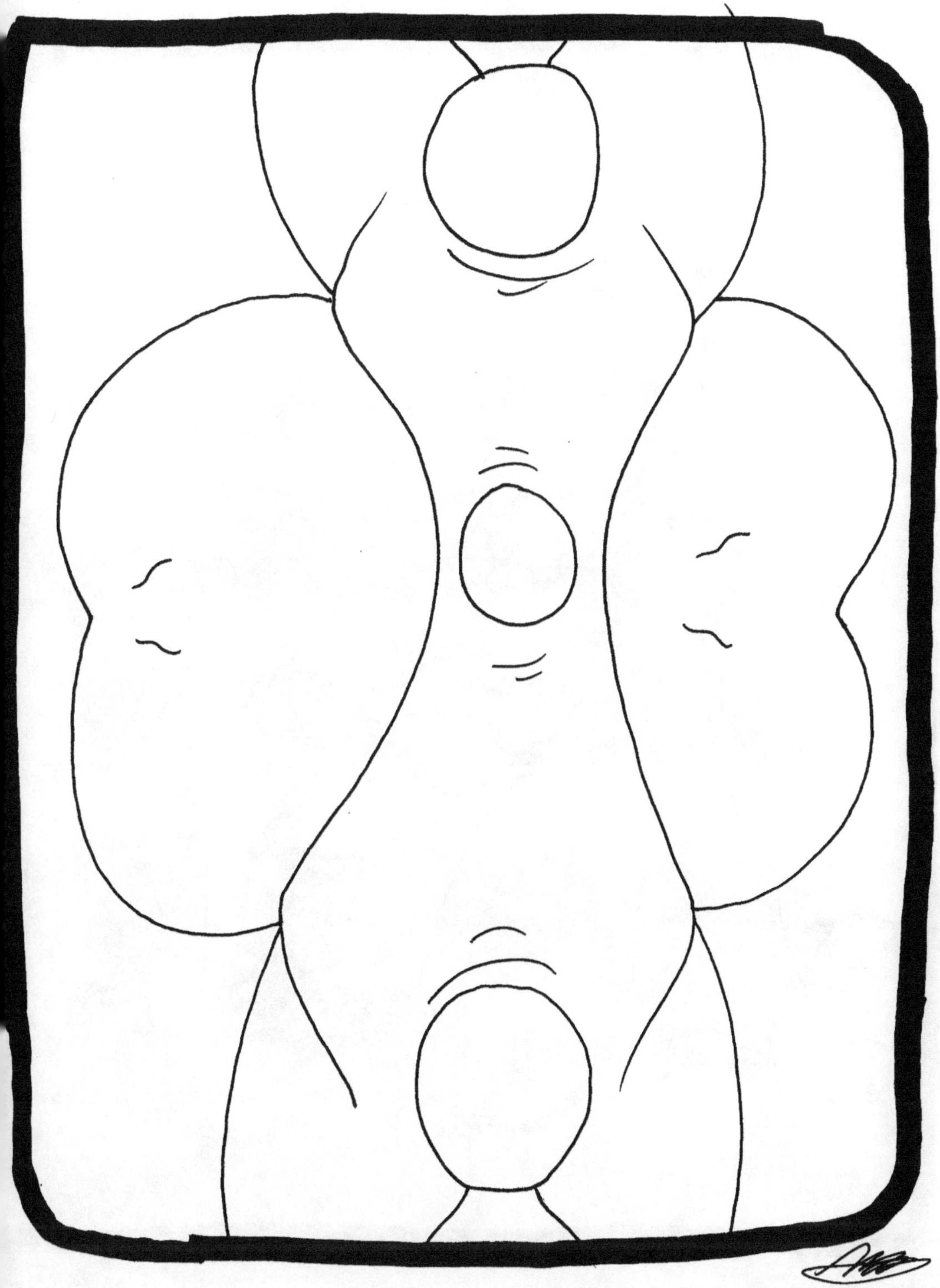

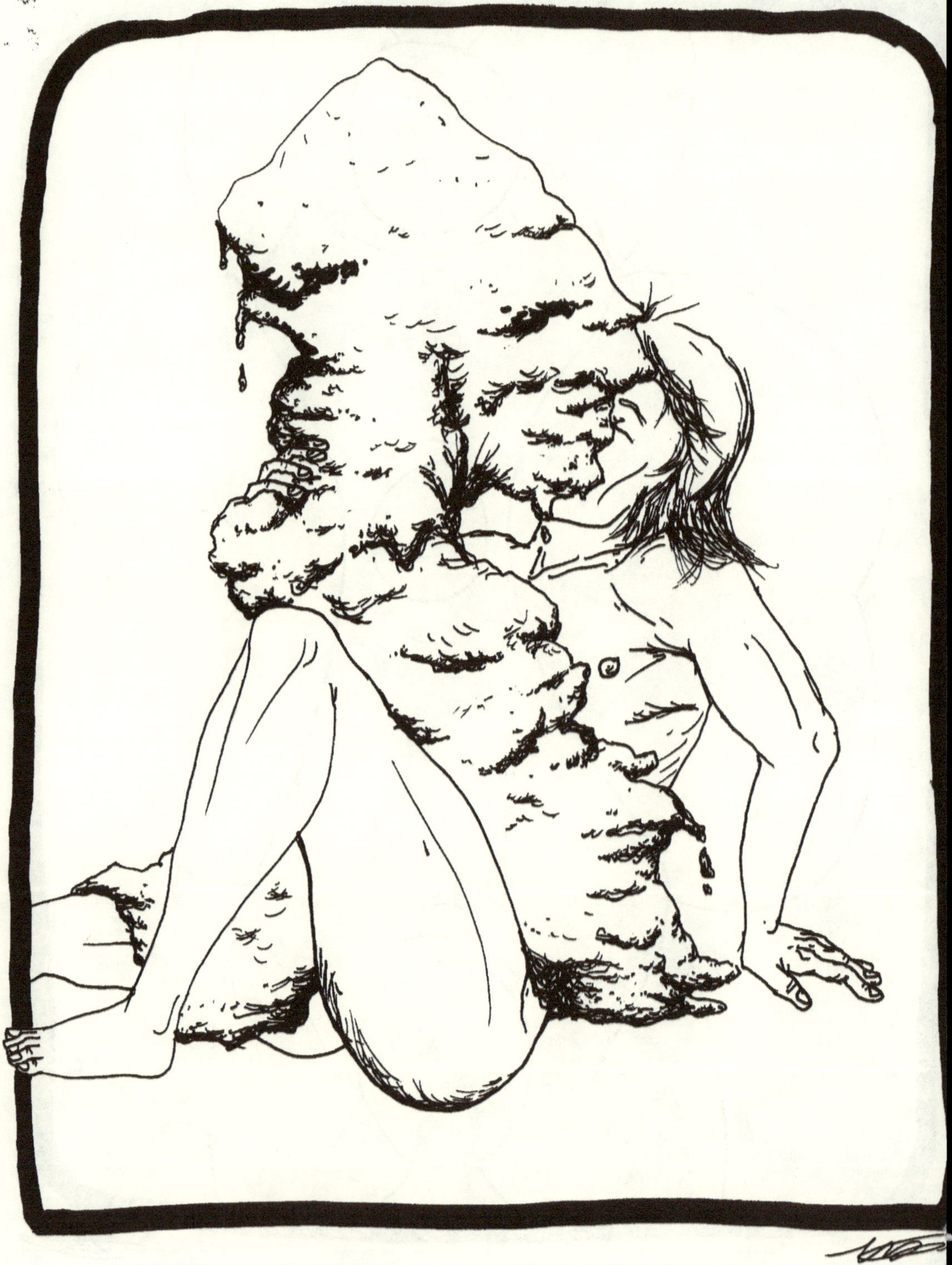

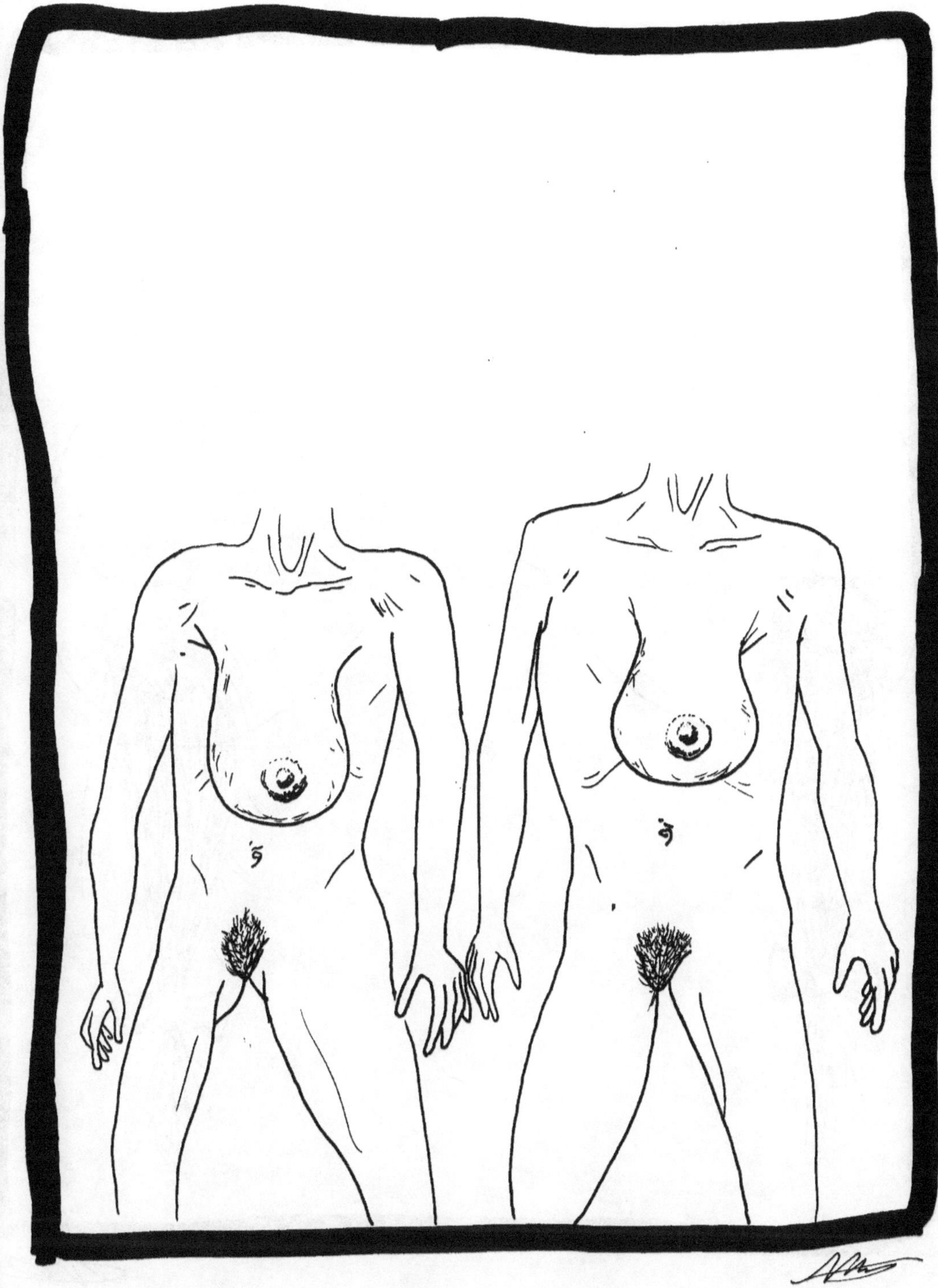

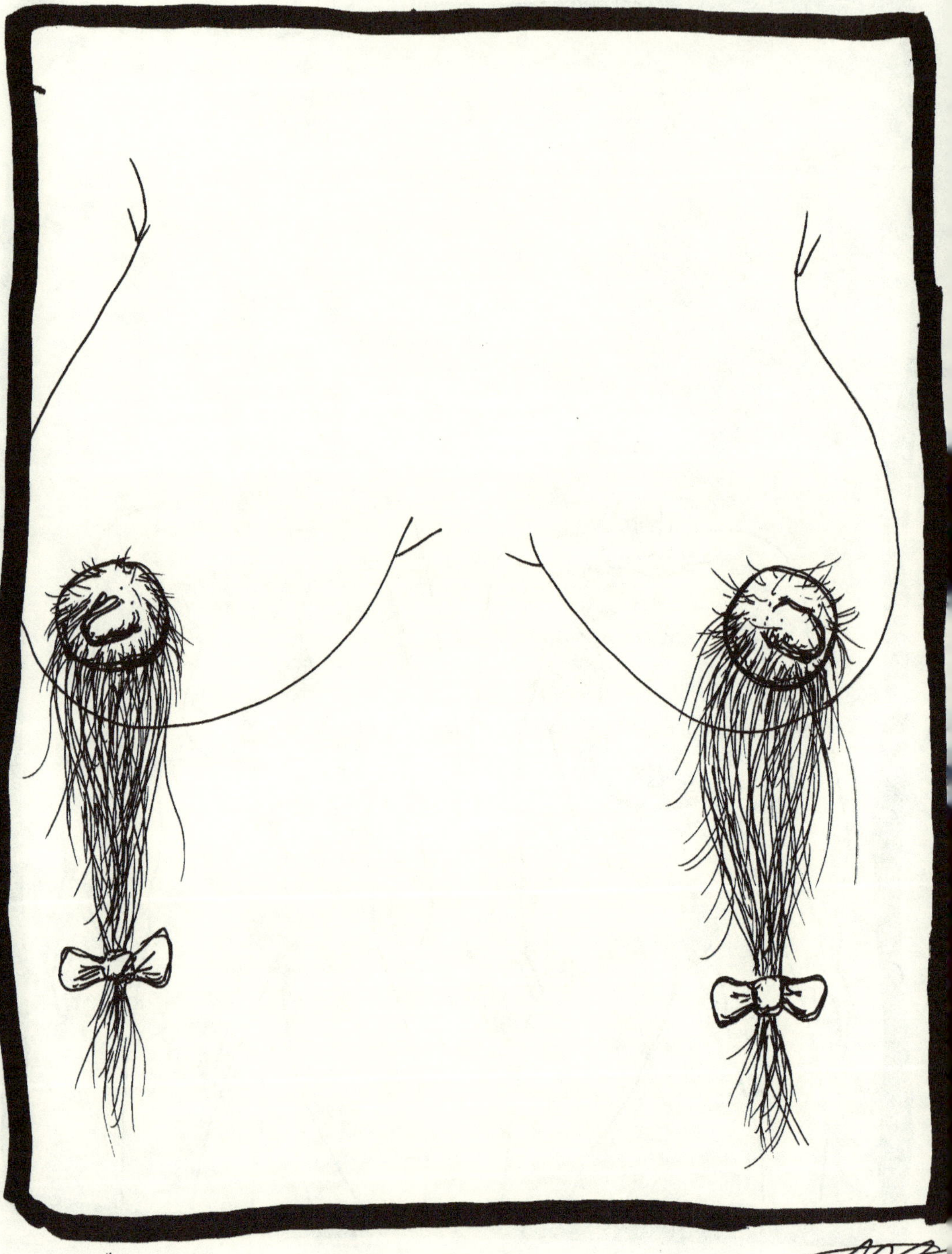

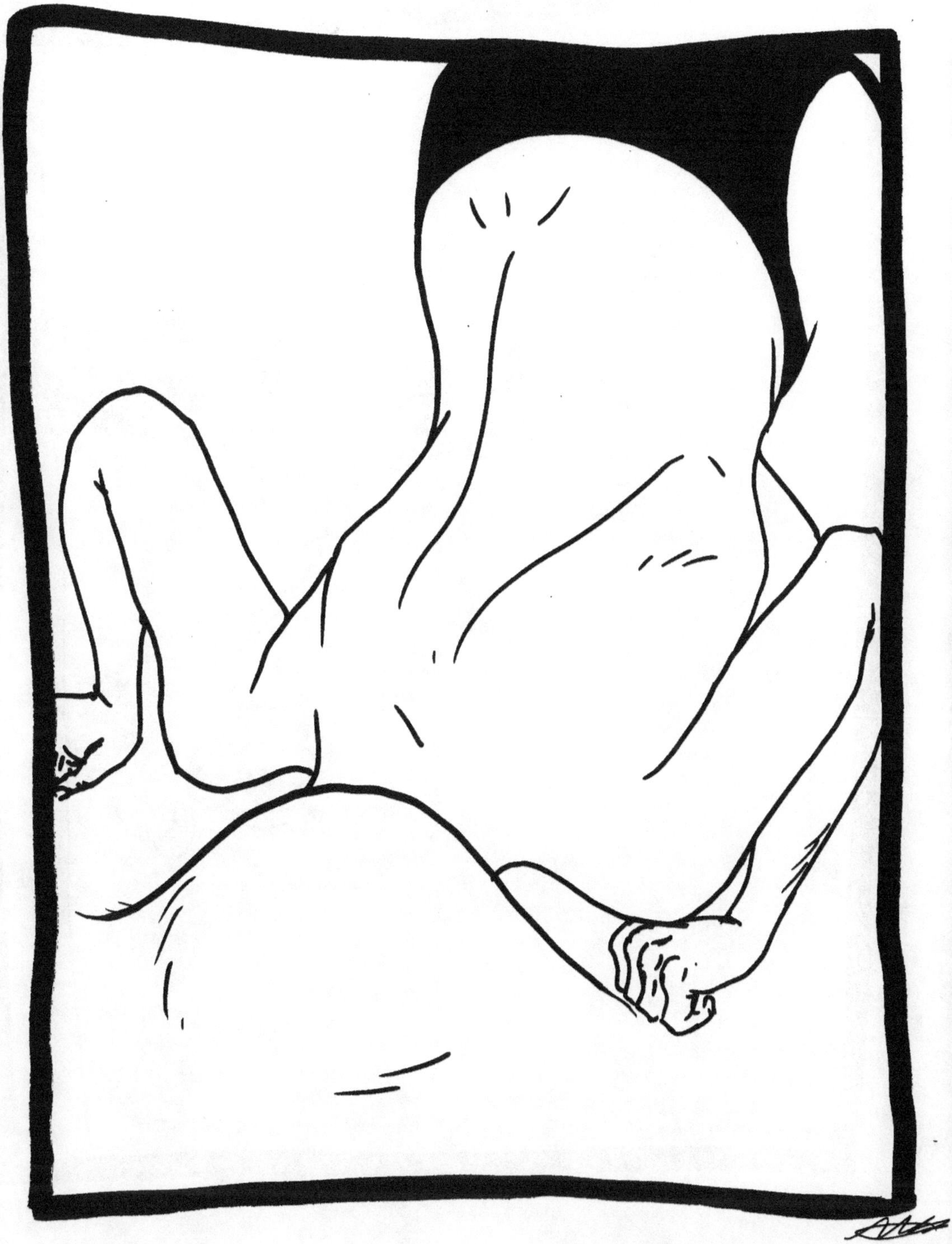

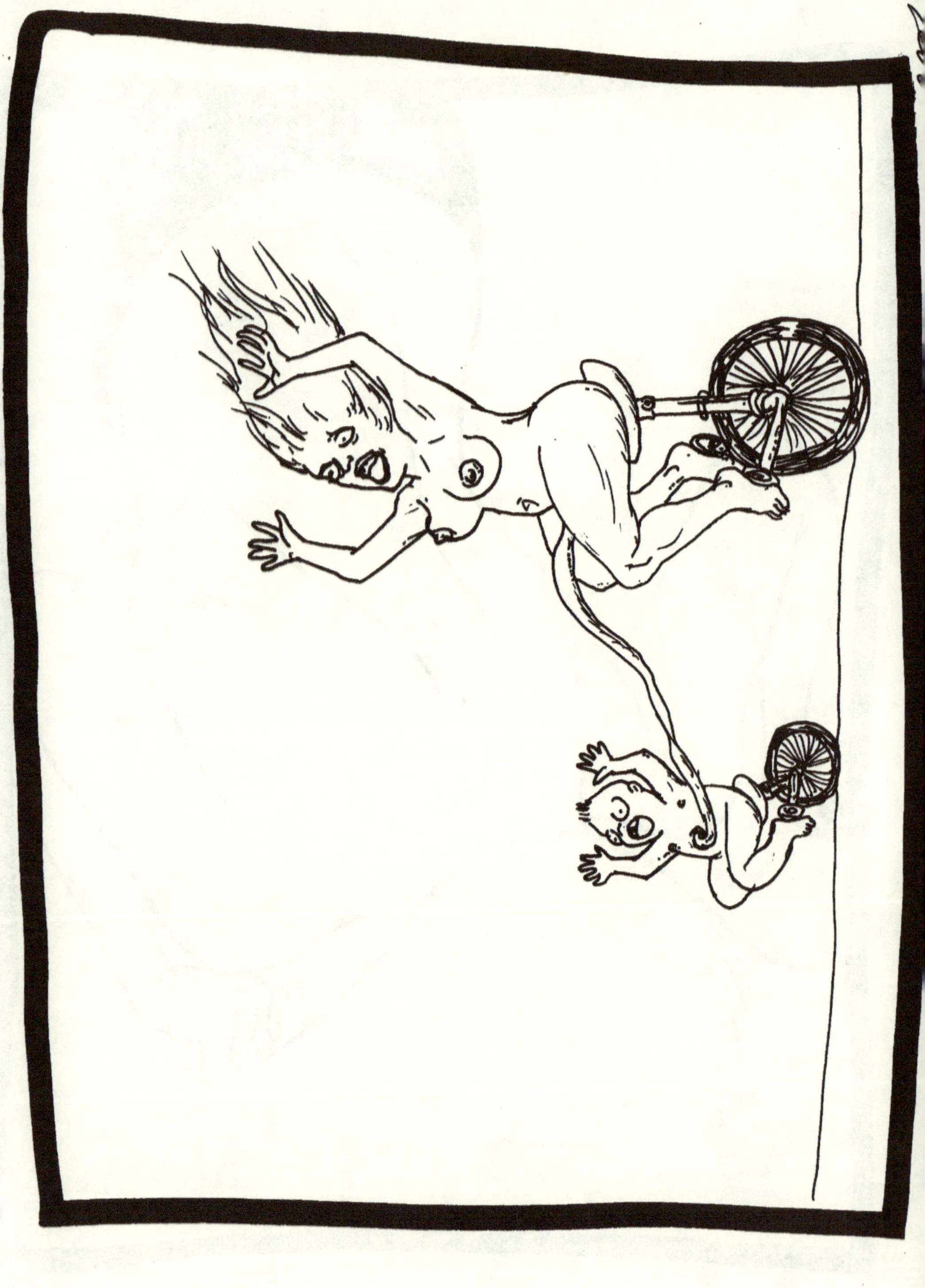

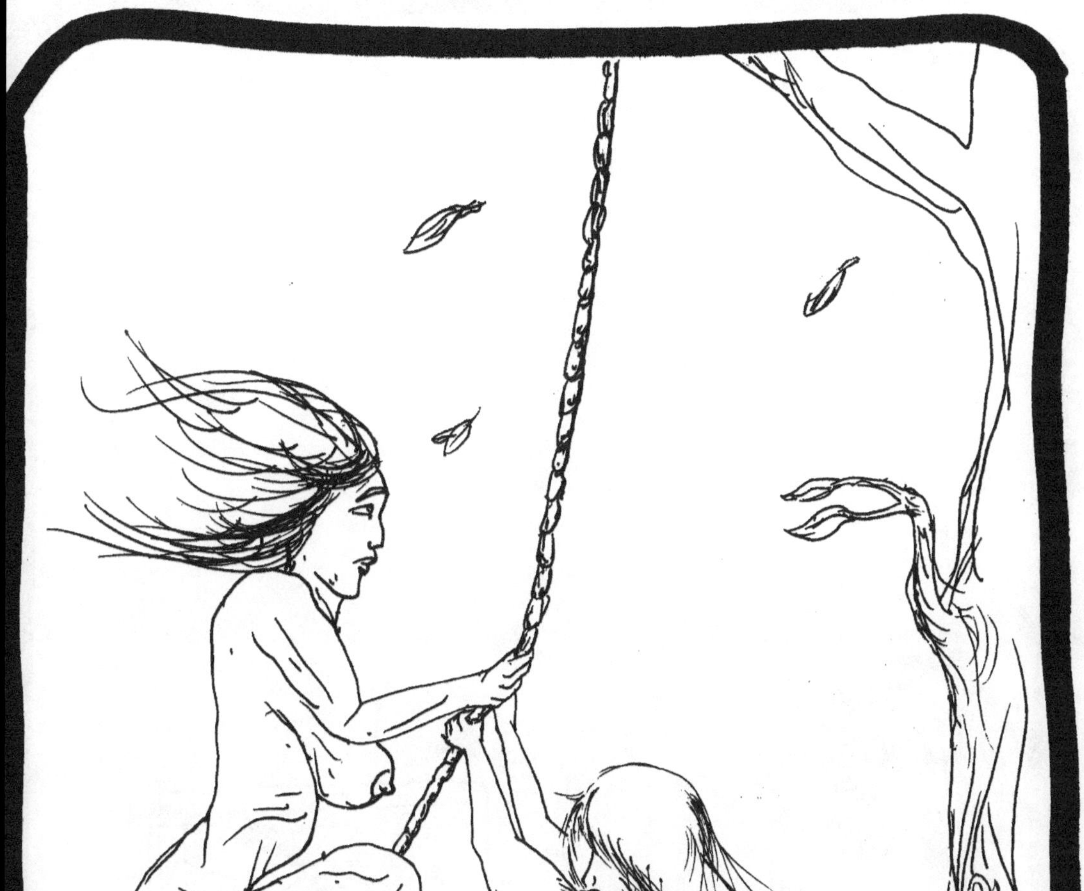

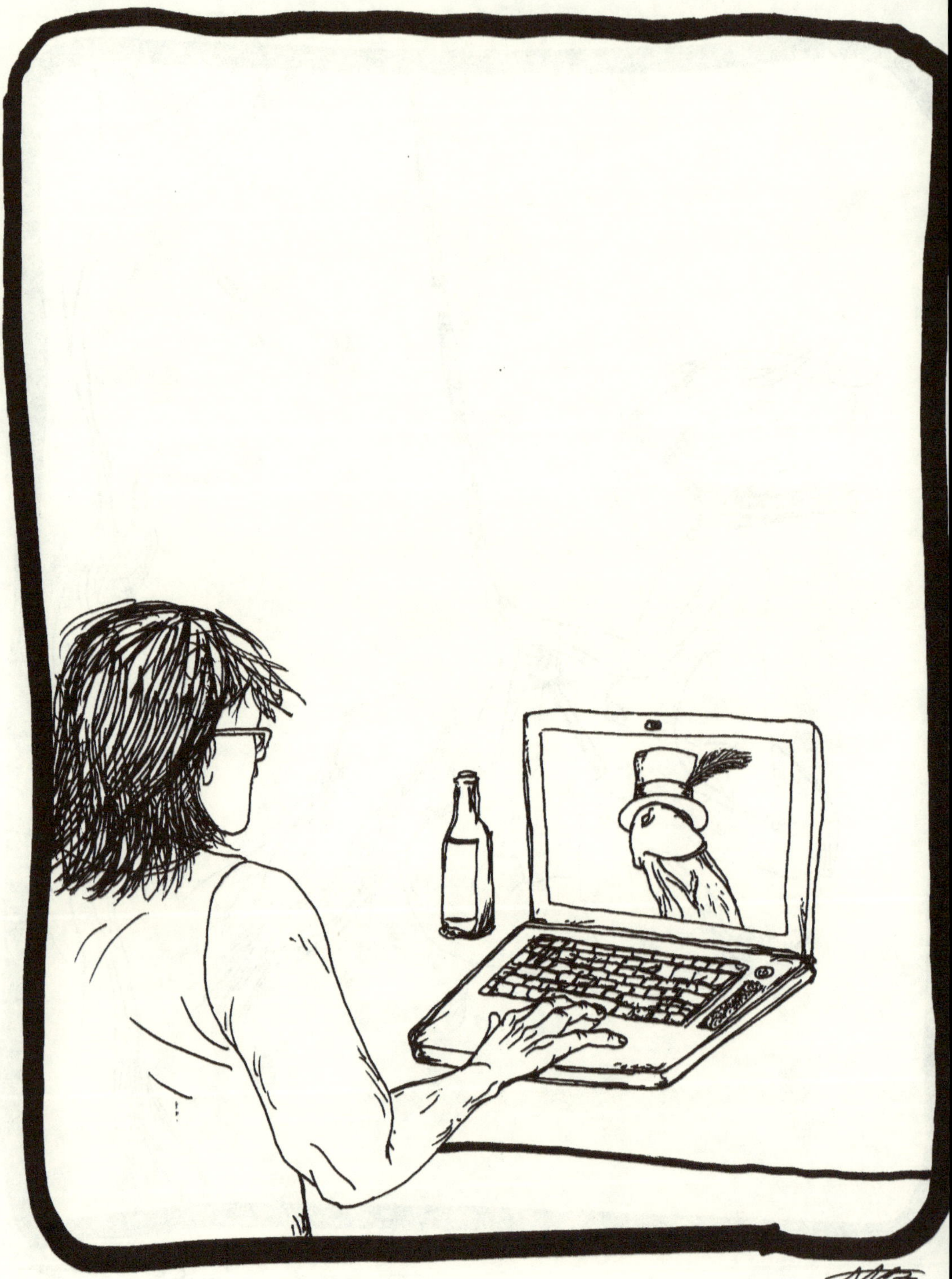

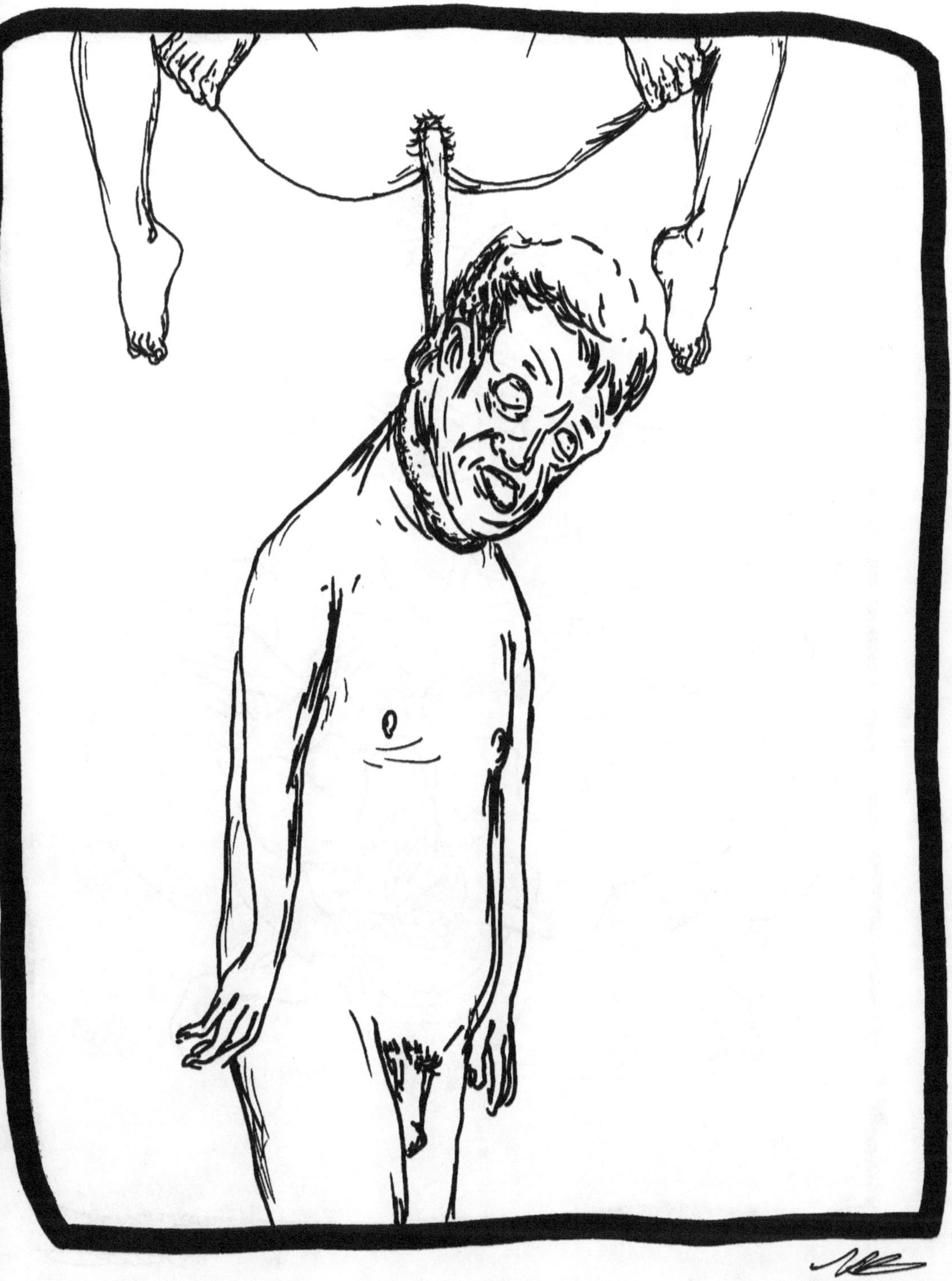

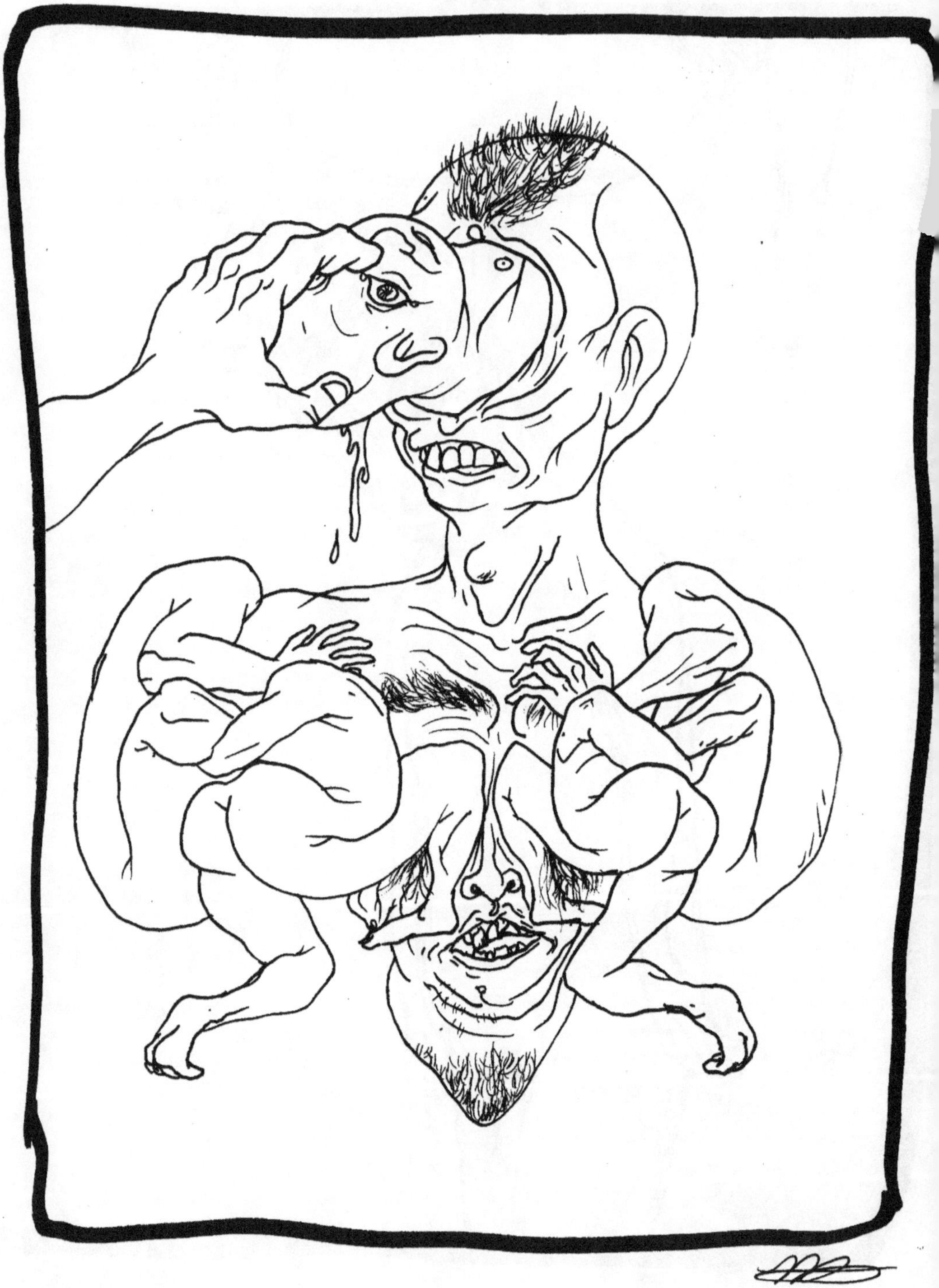

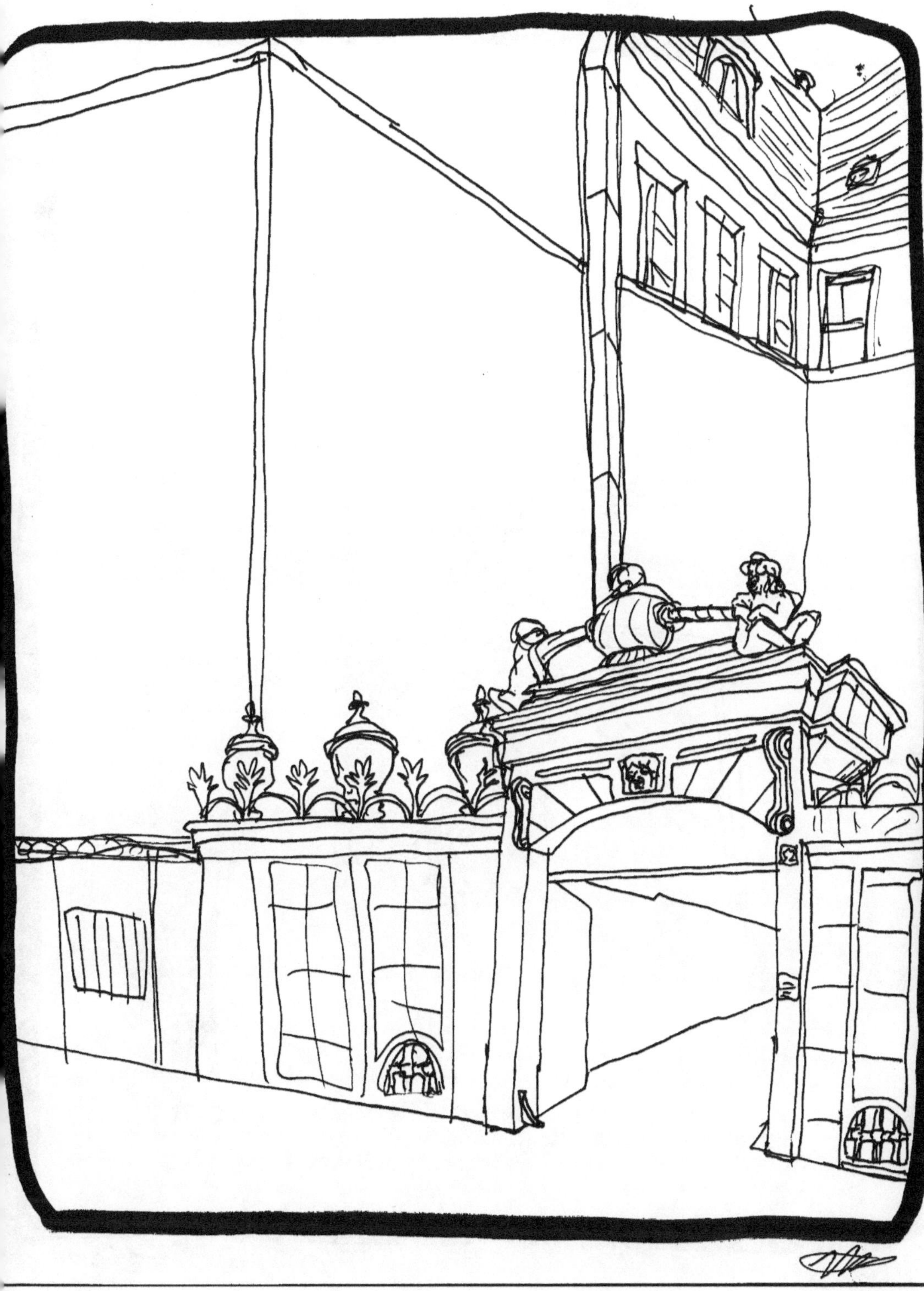

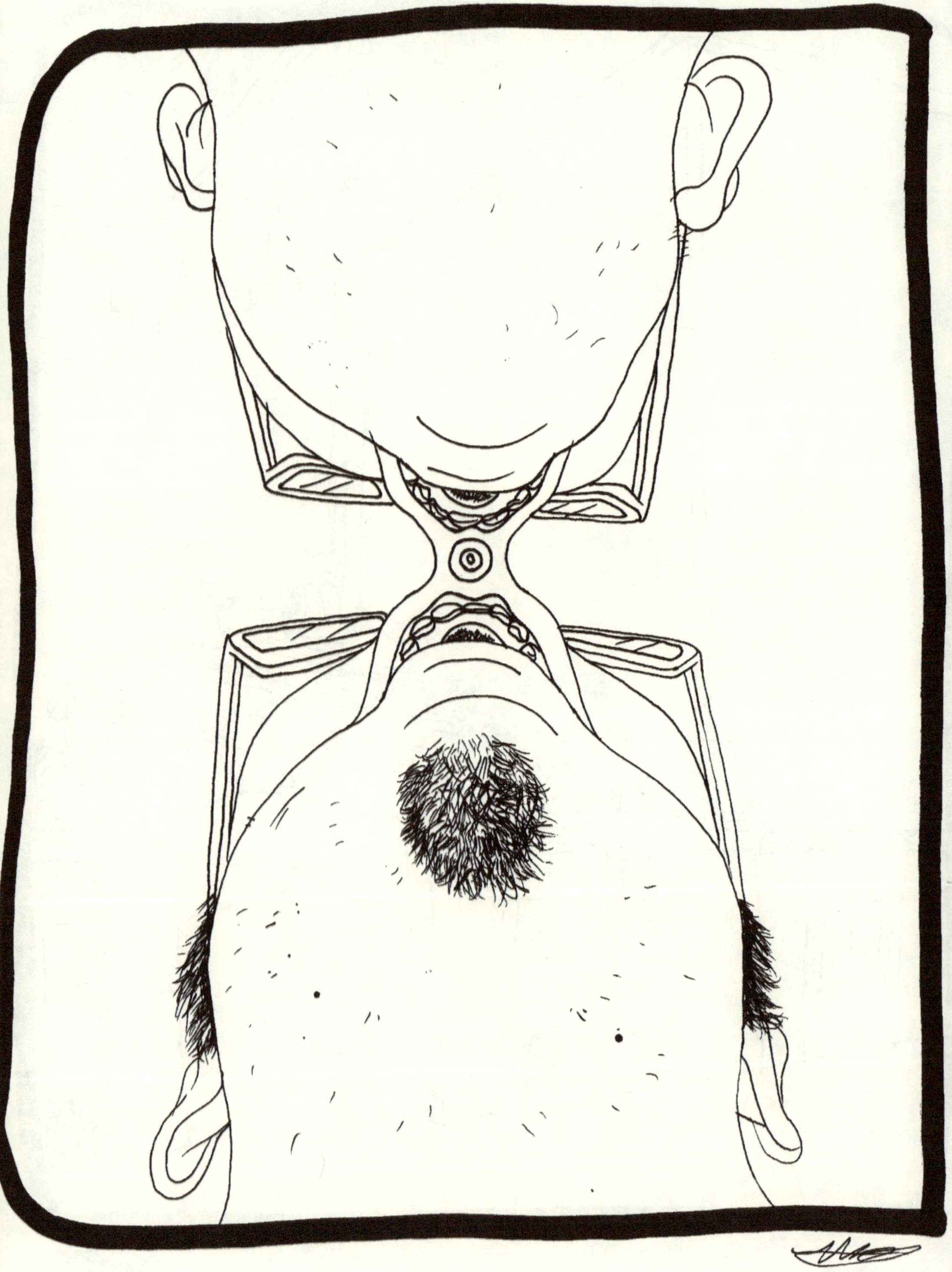

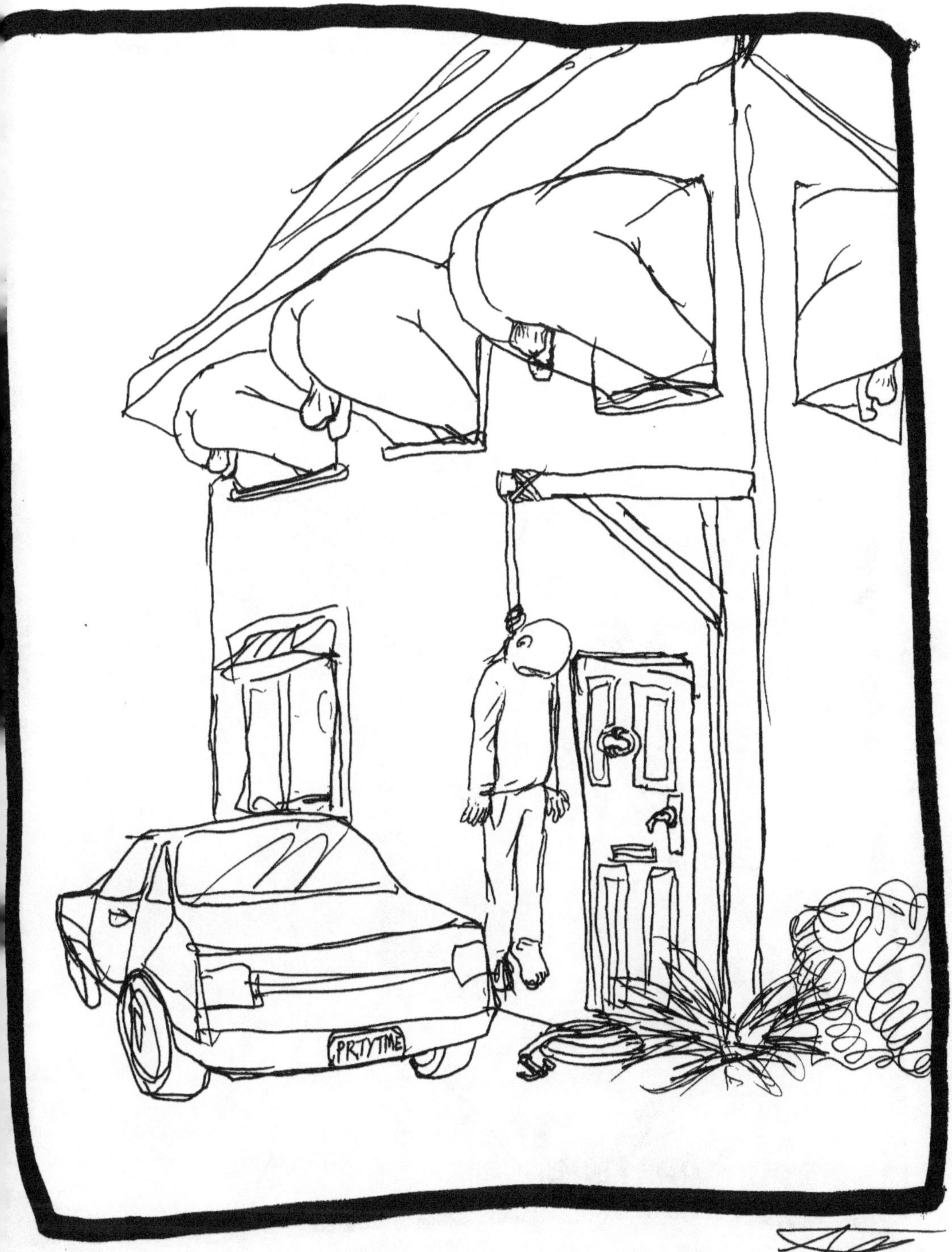
PRTYTME

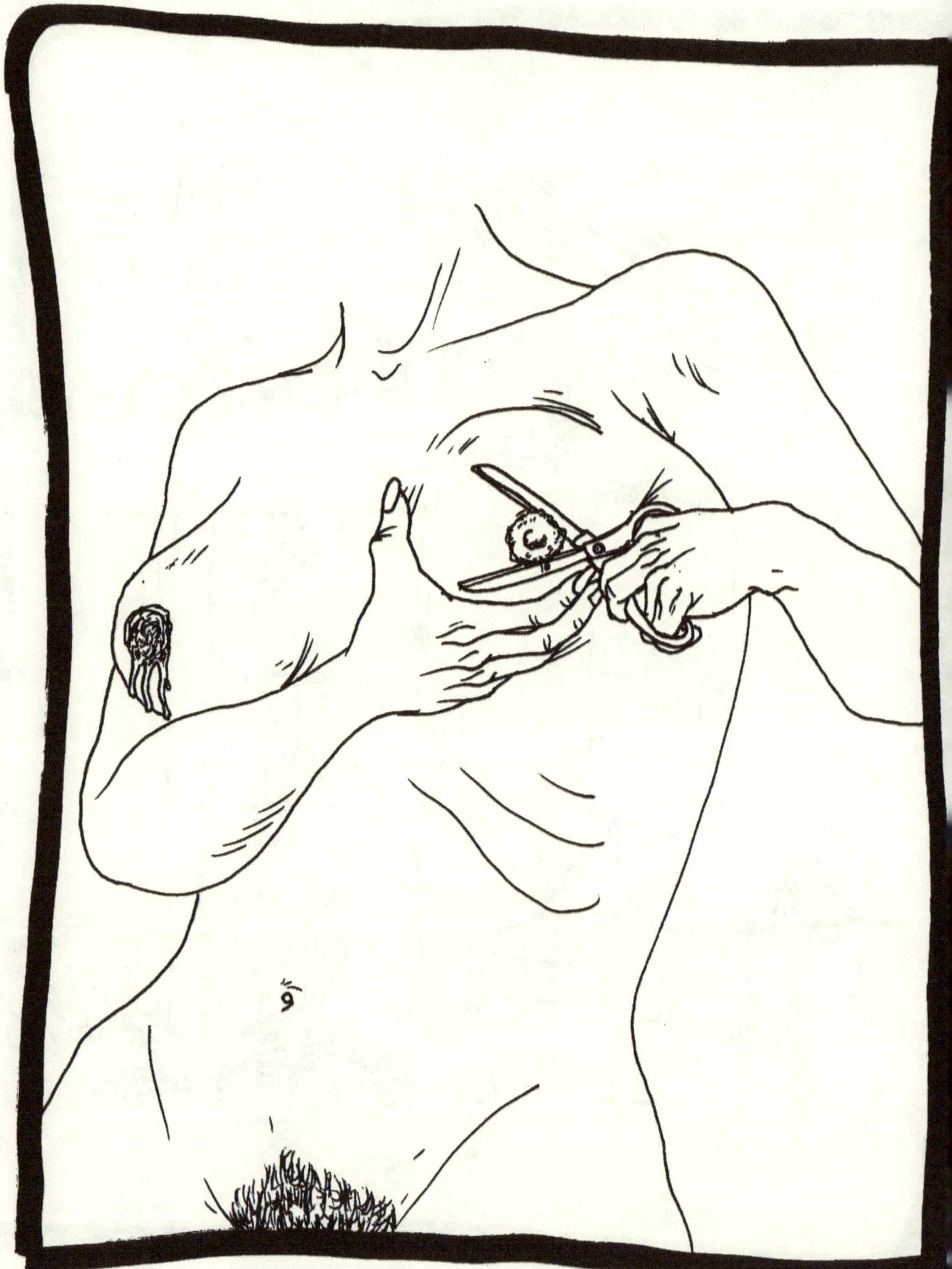

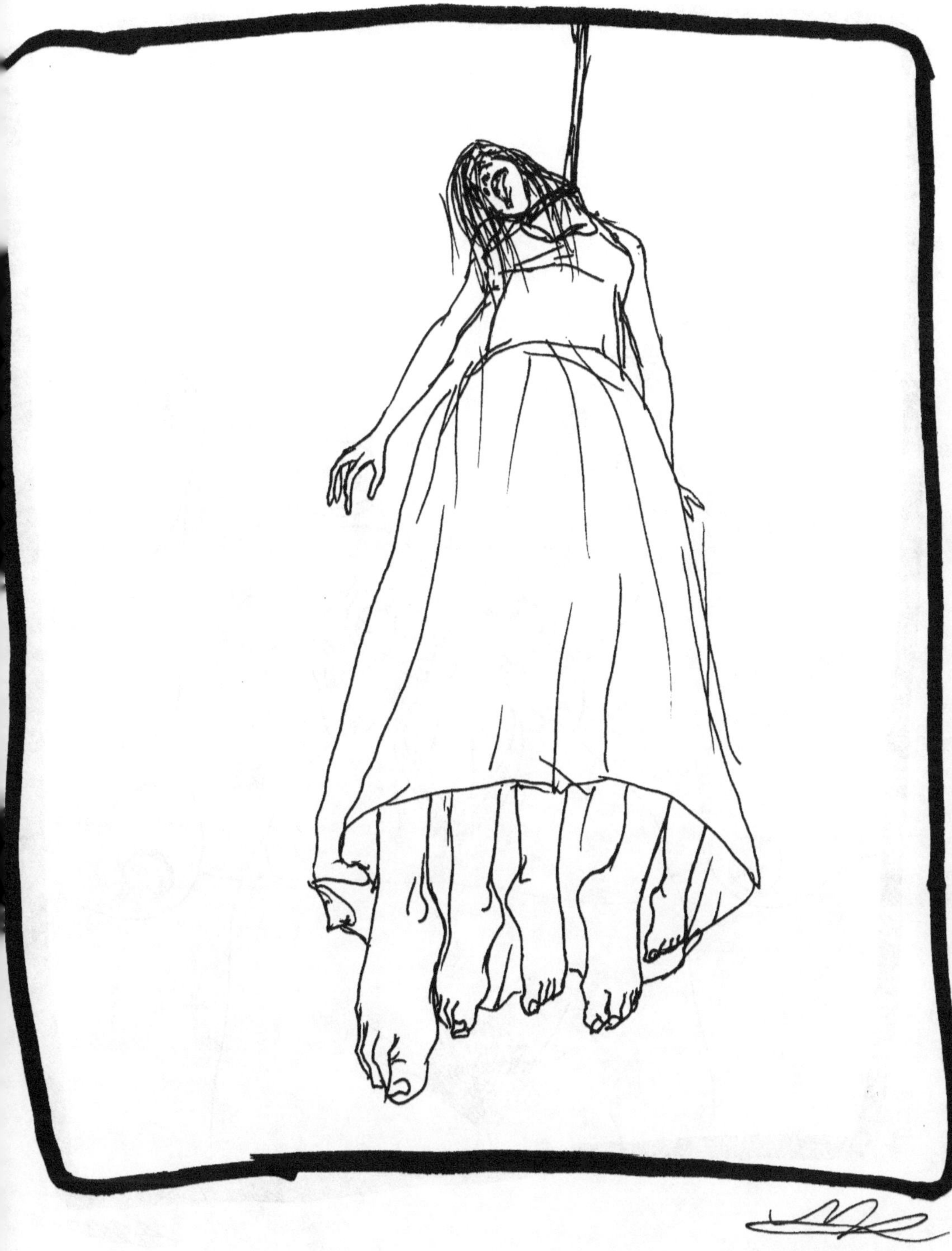

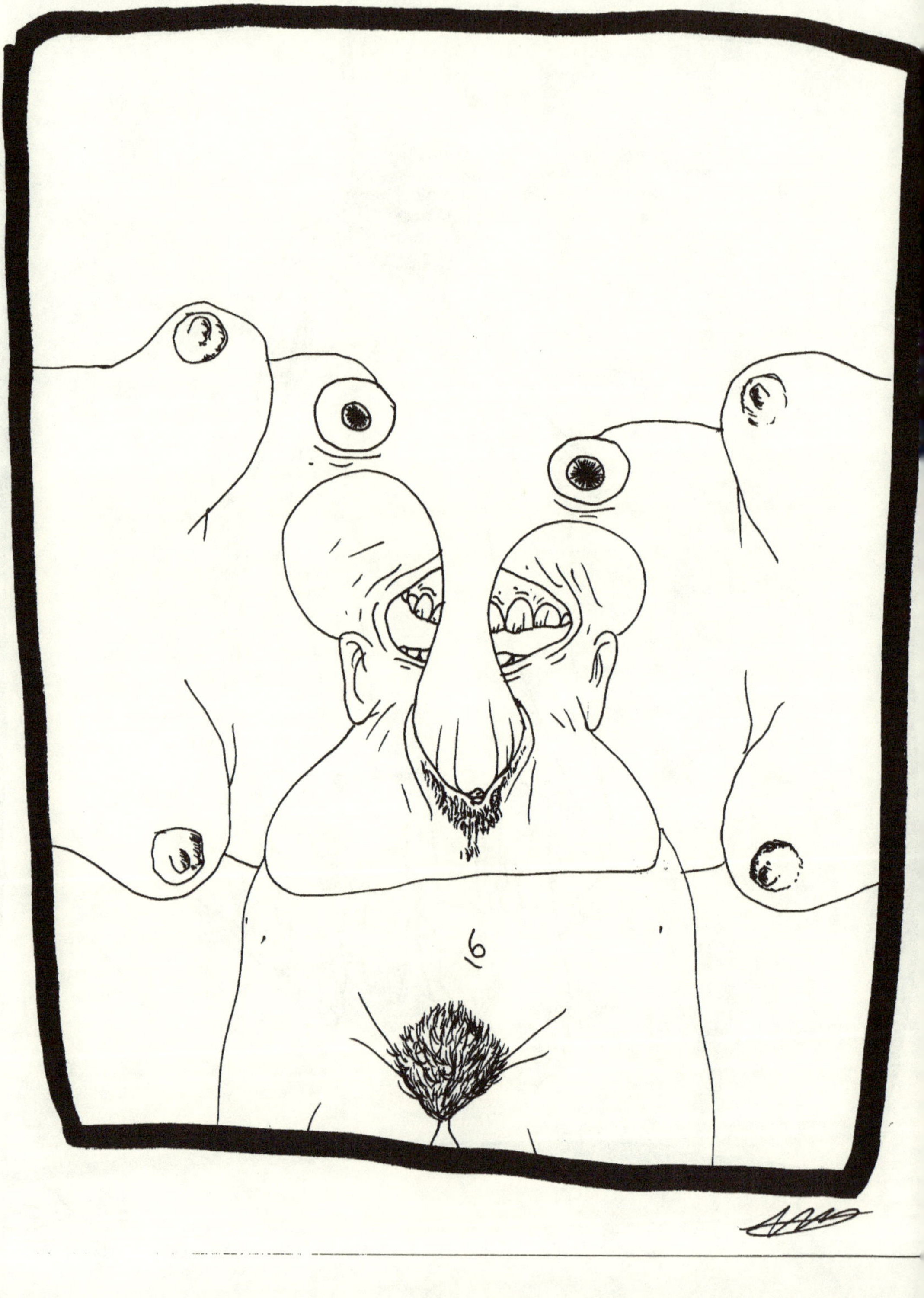

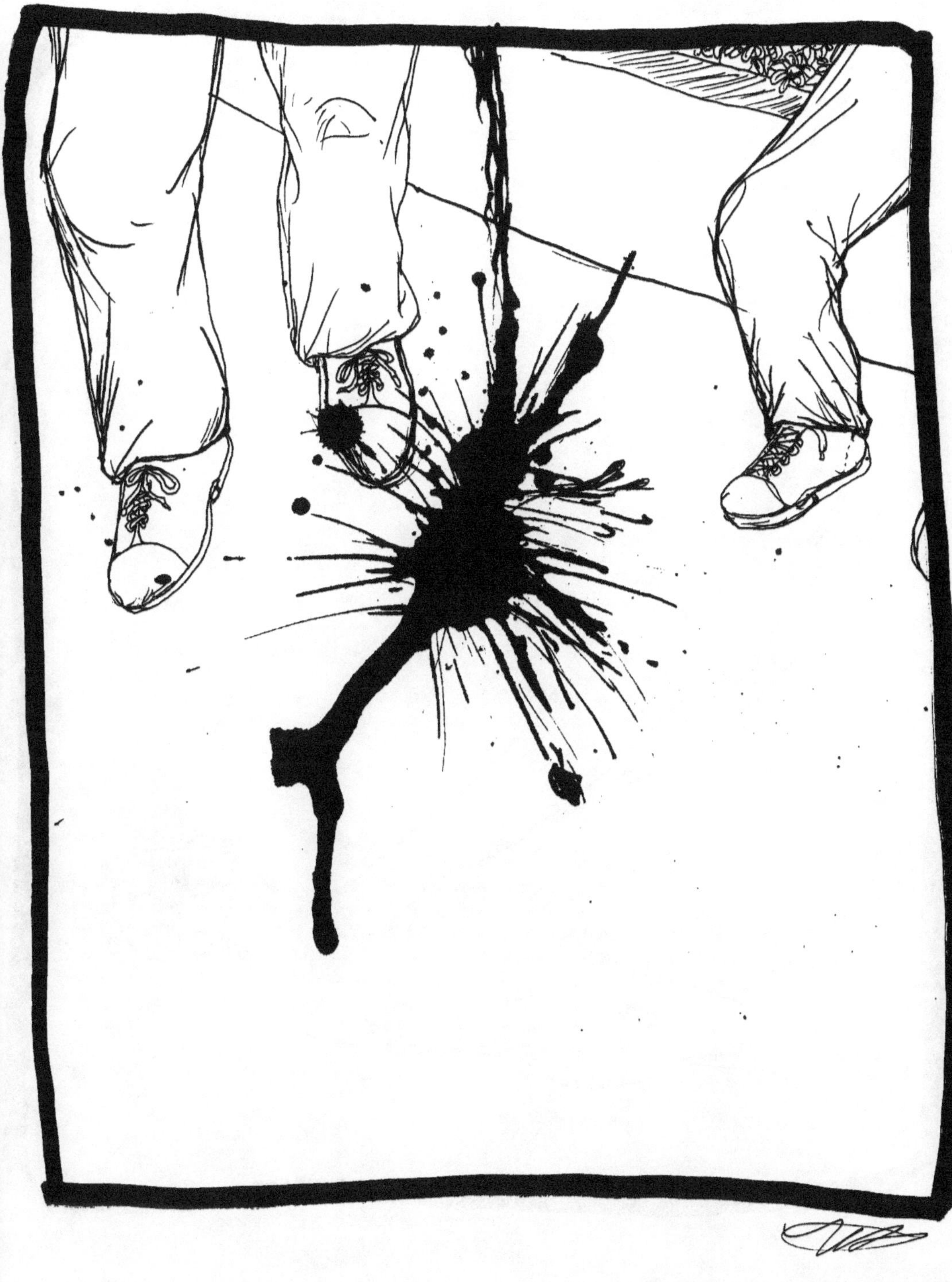

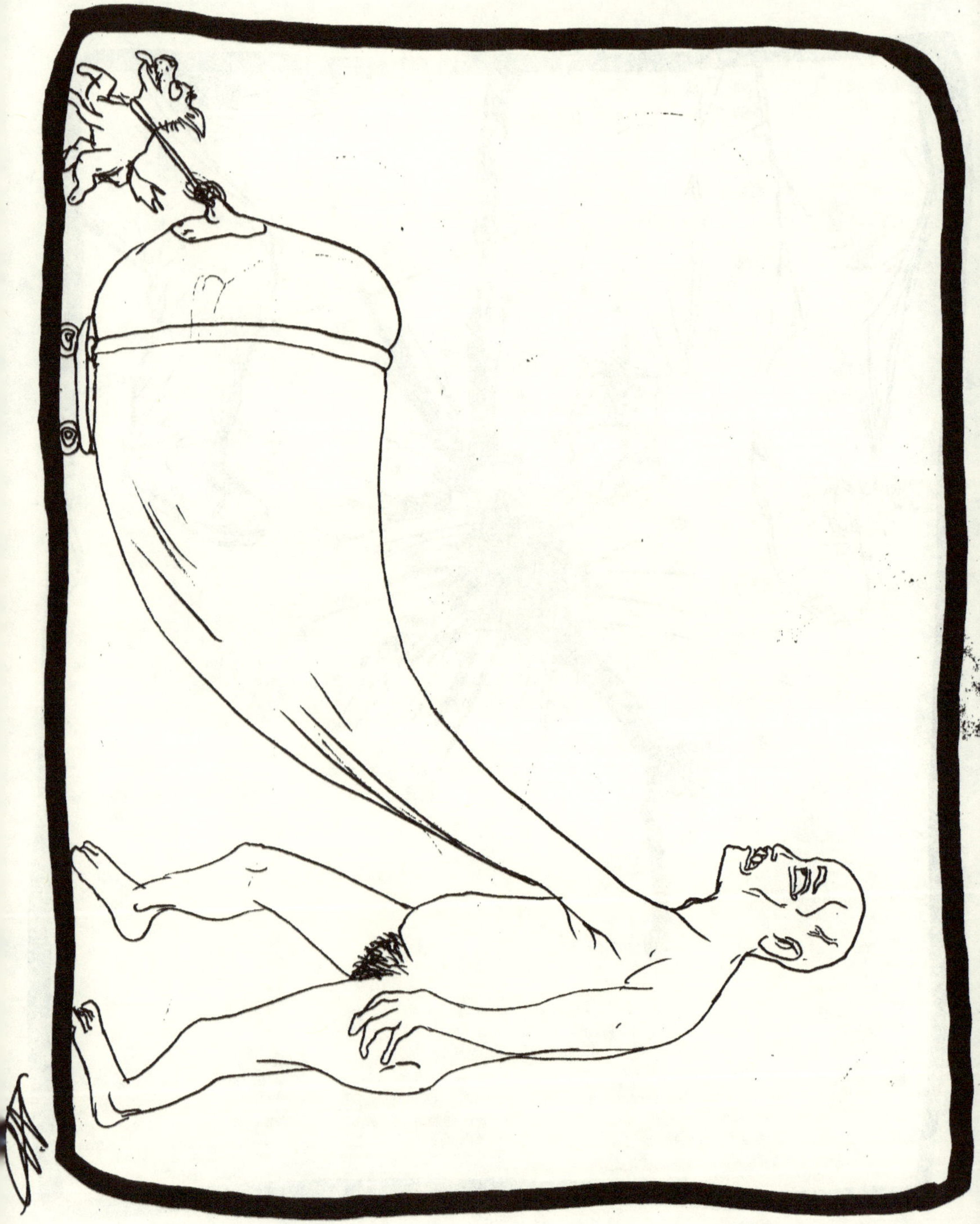

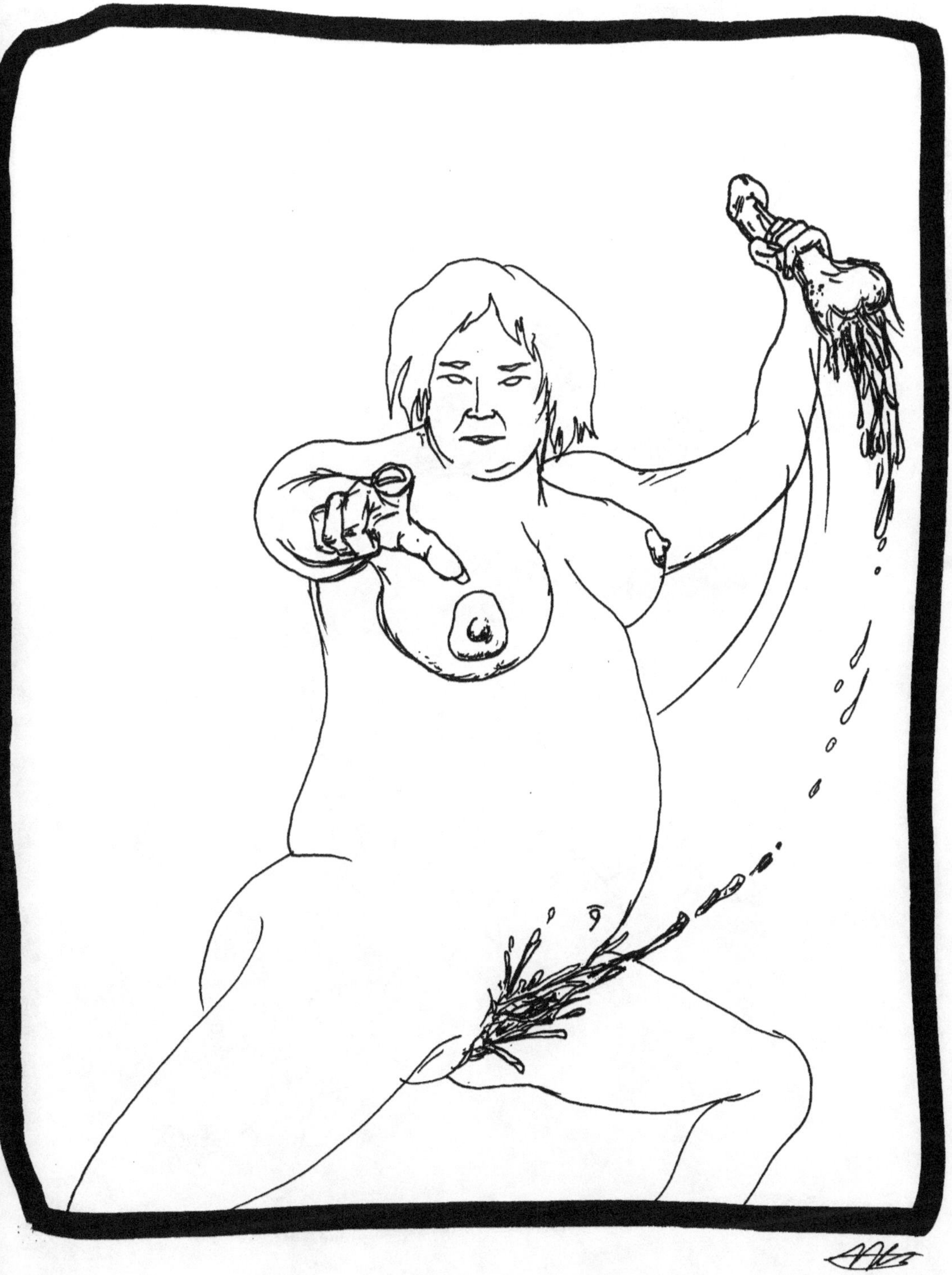

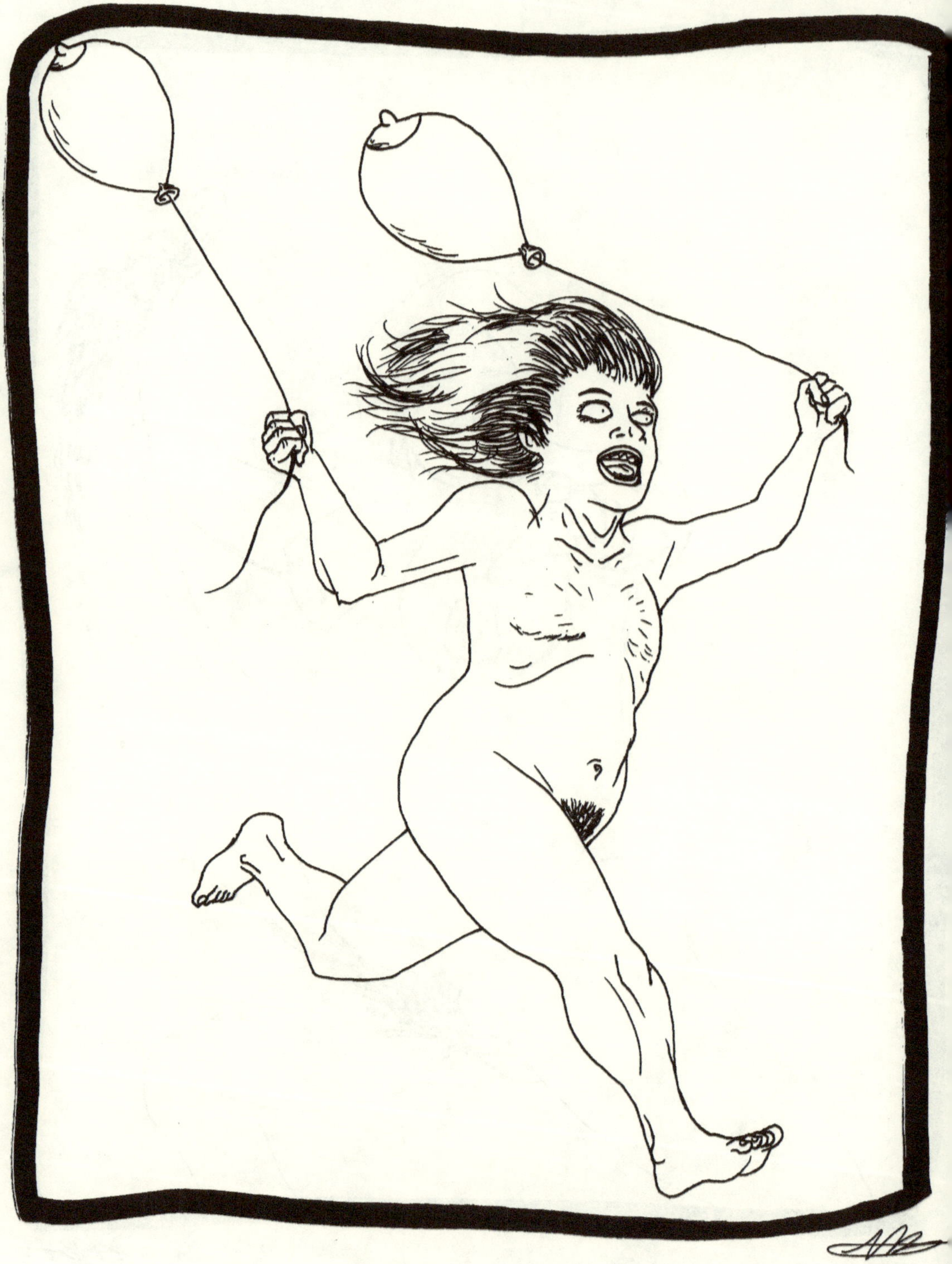

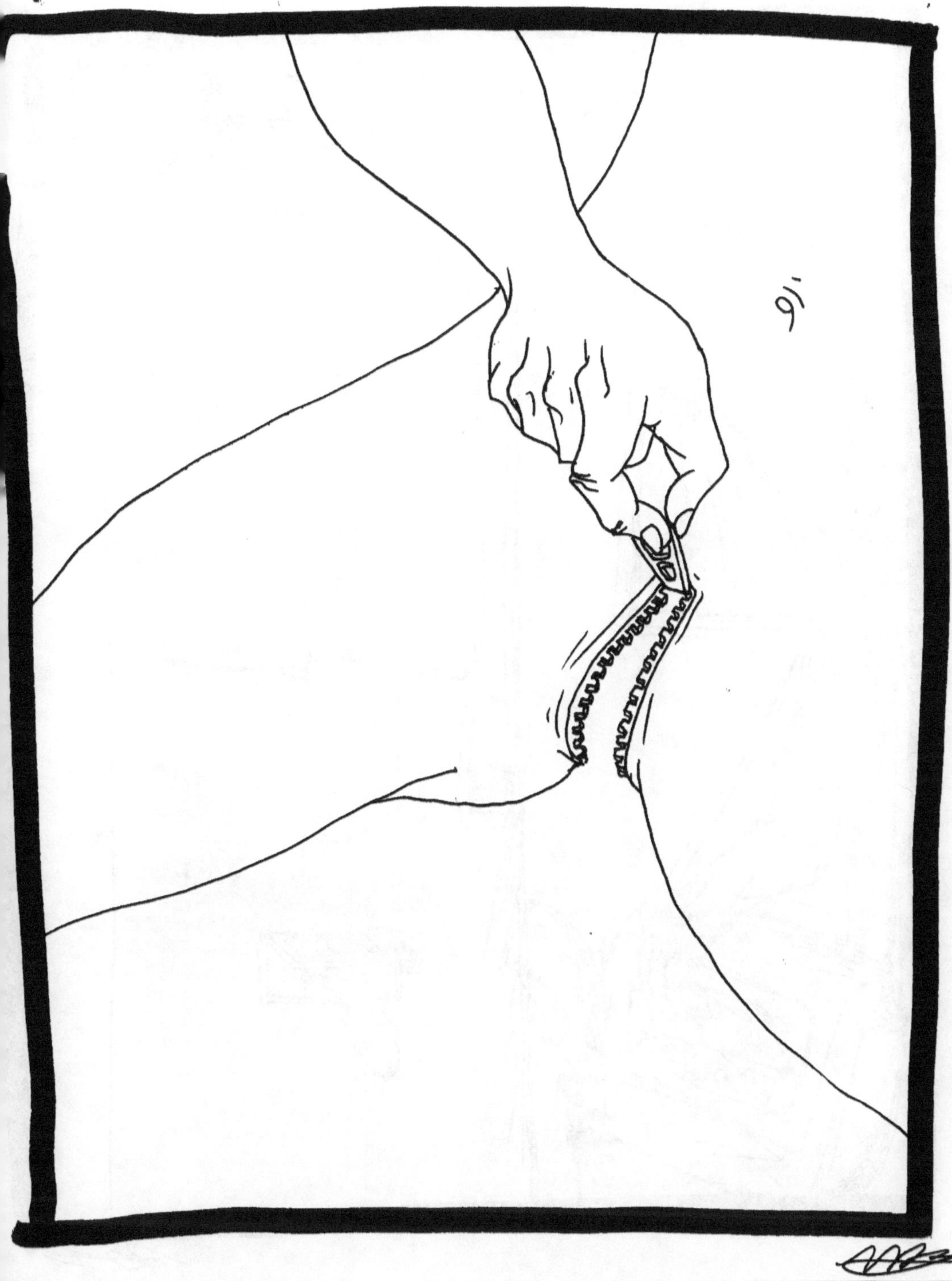

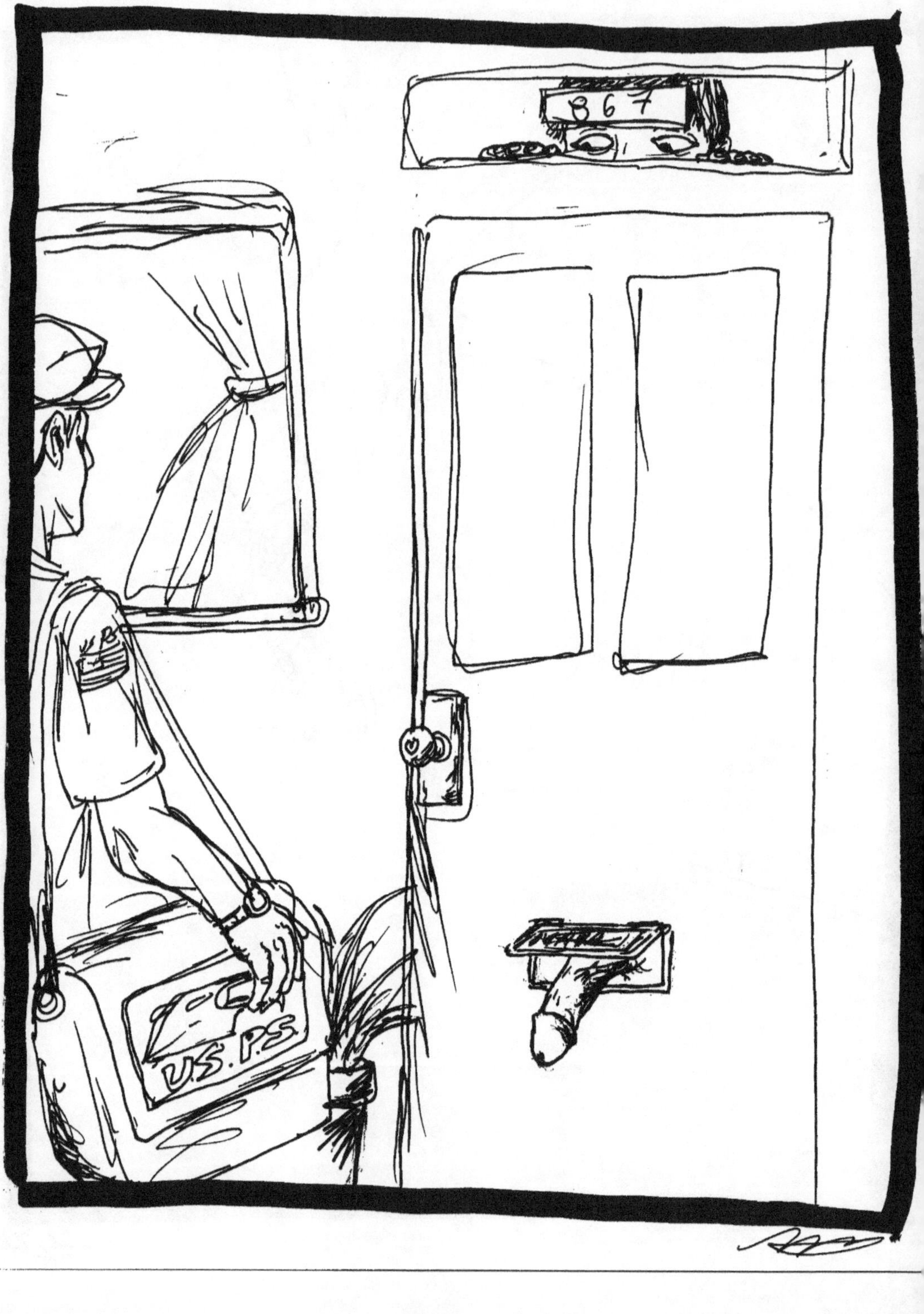
867
U.S.P.S.

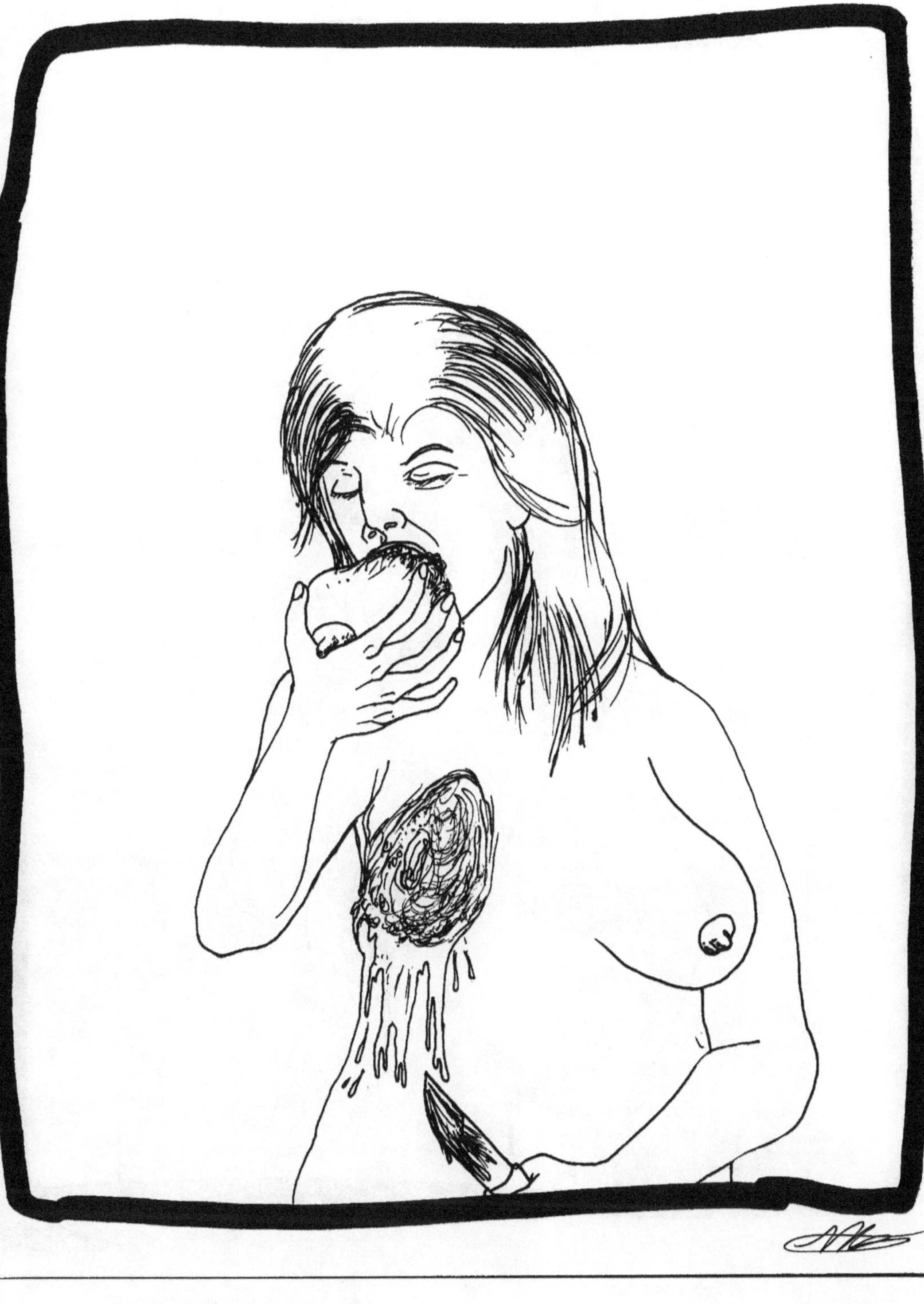

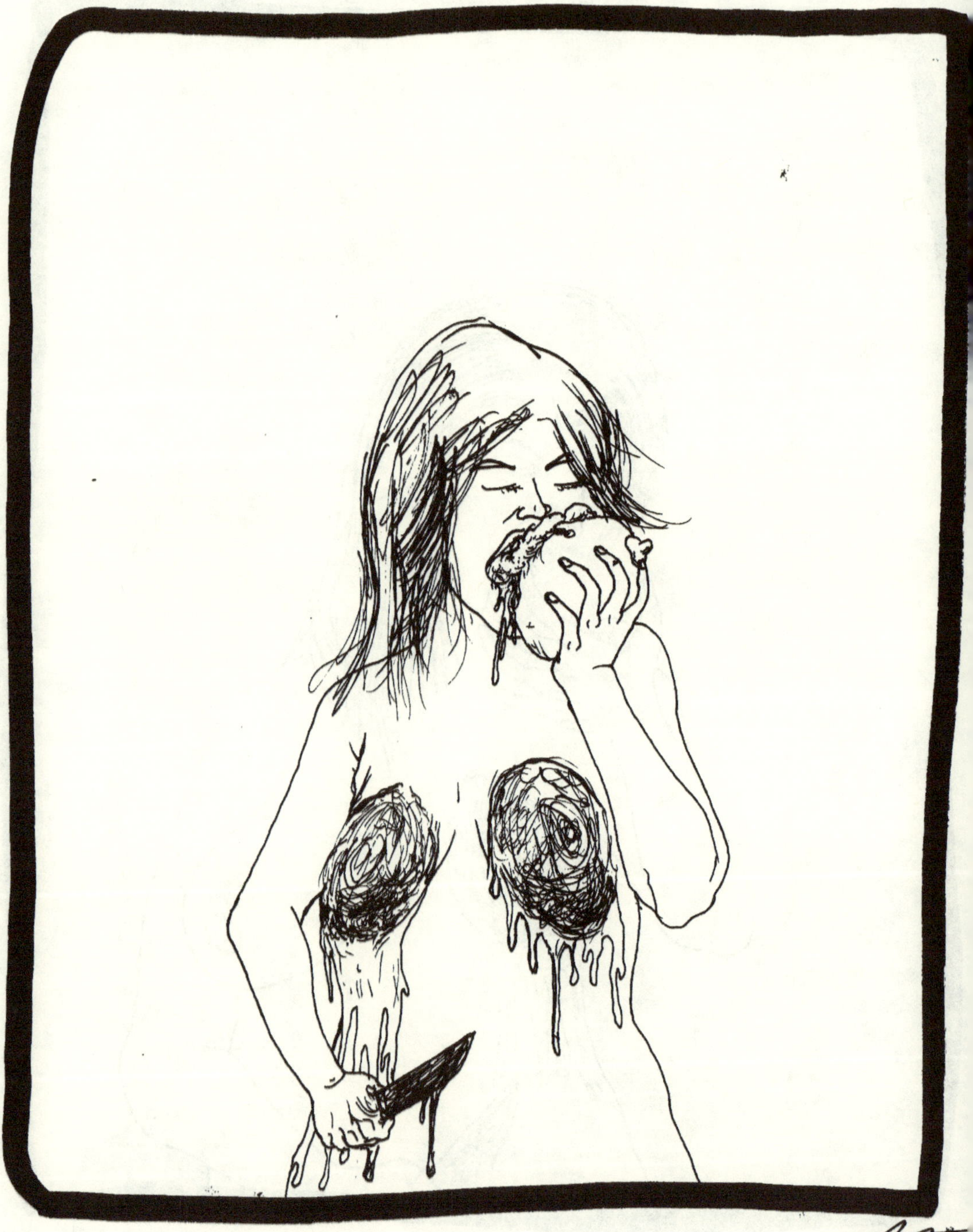

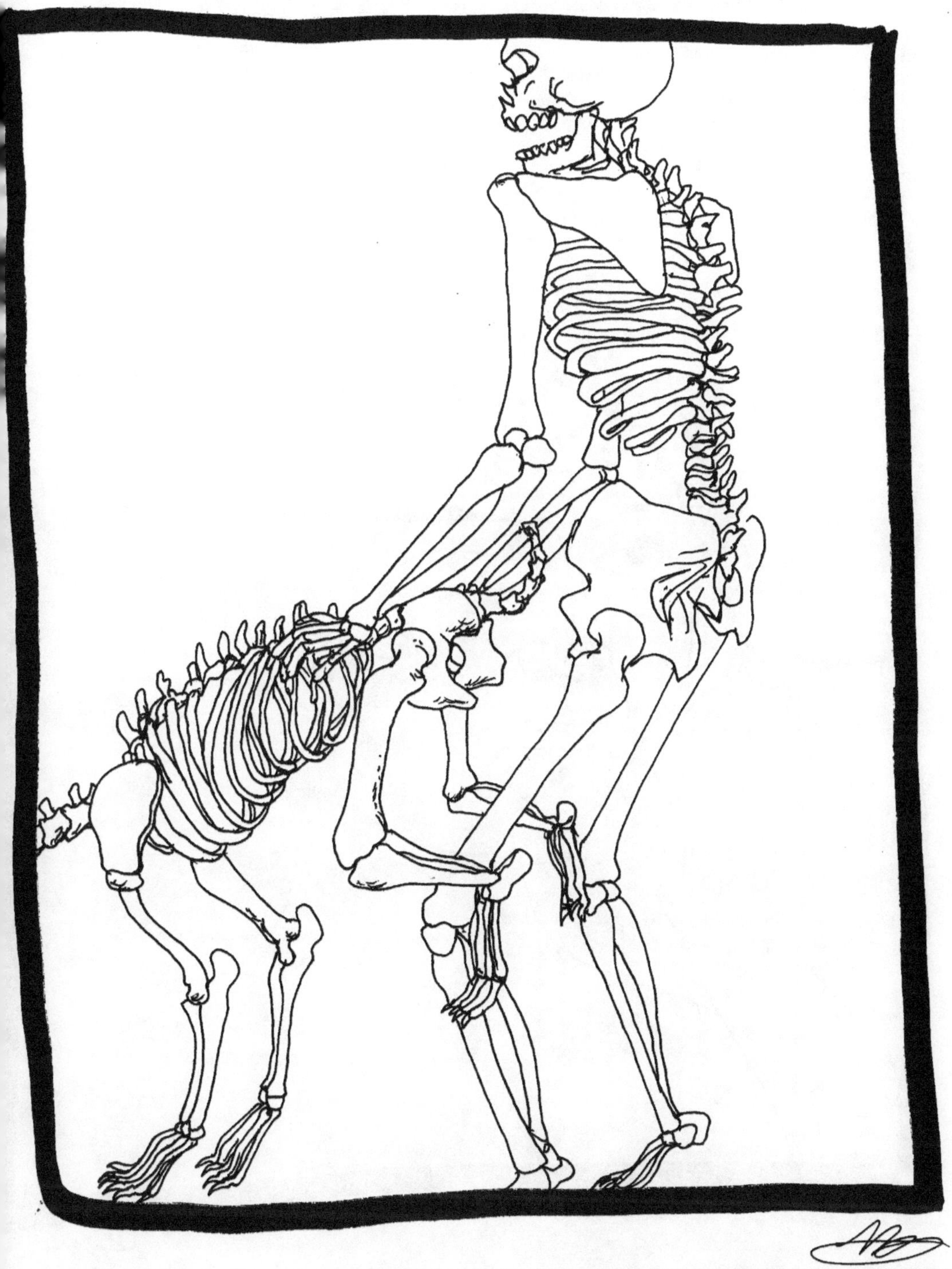

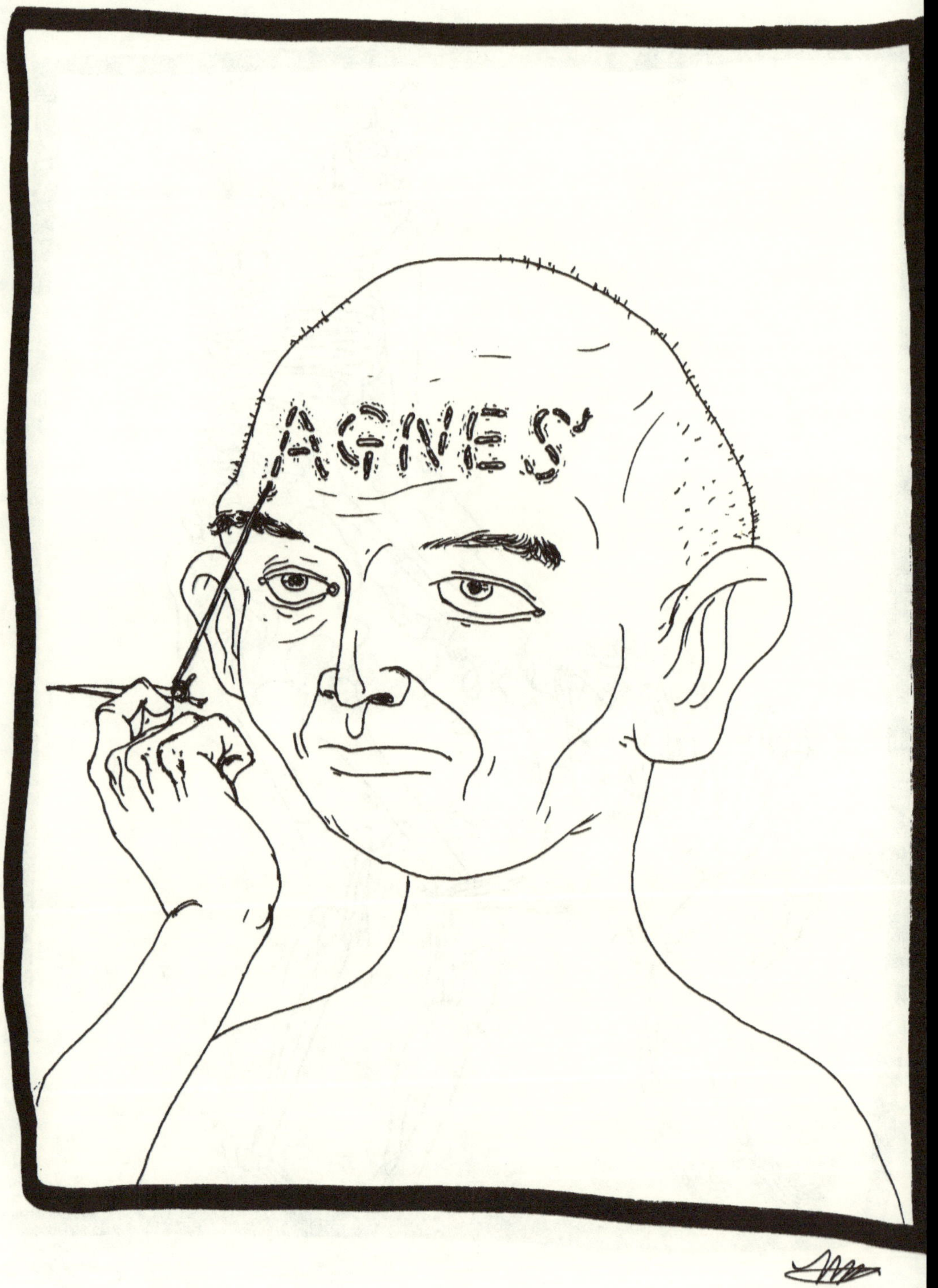
AGNES

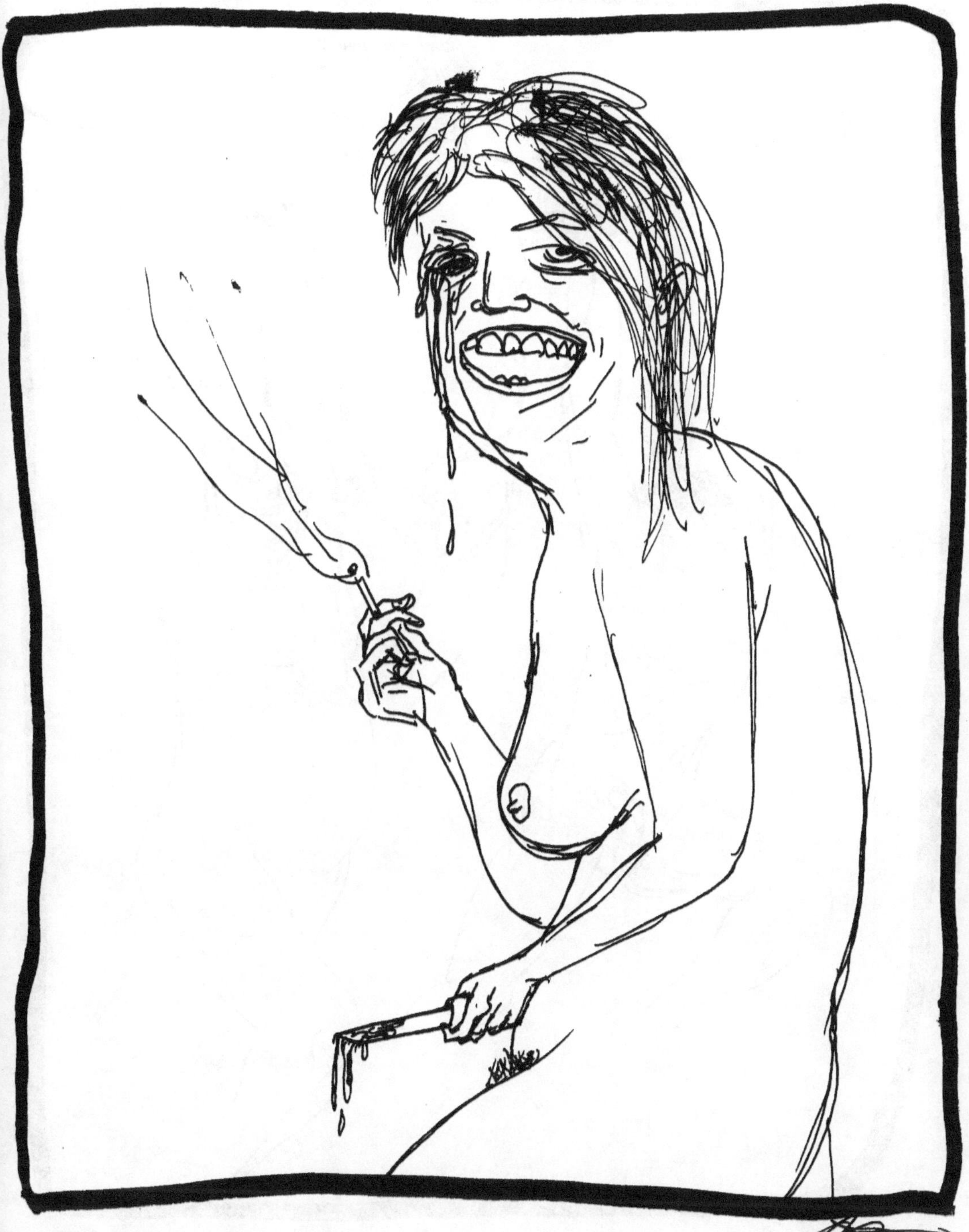

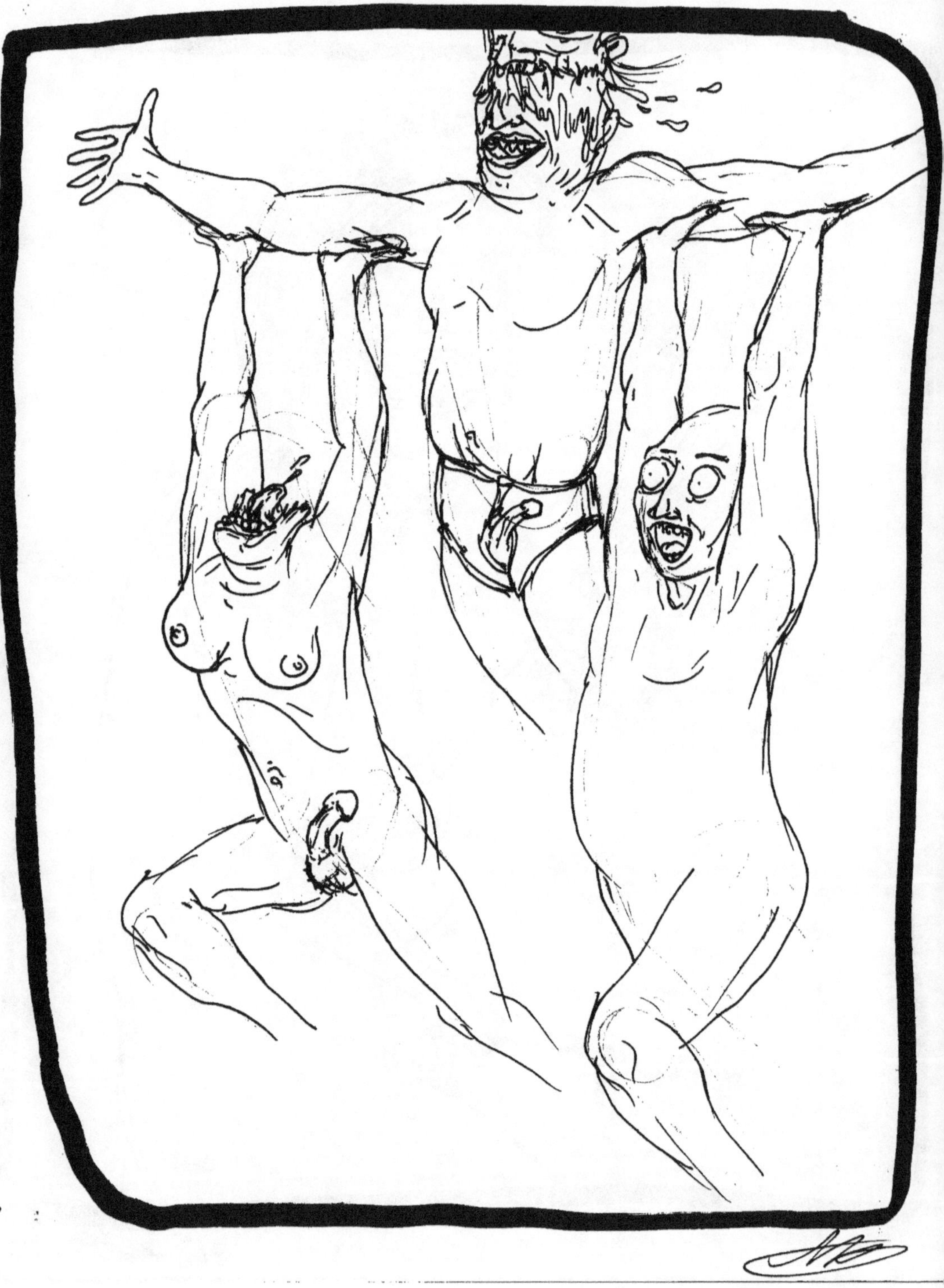

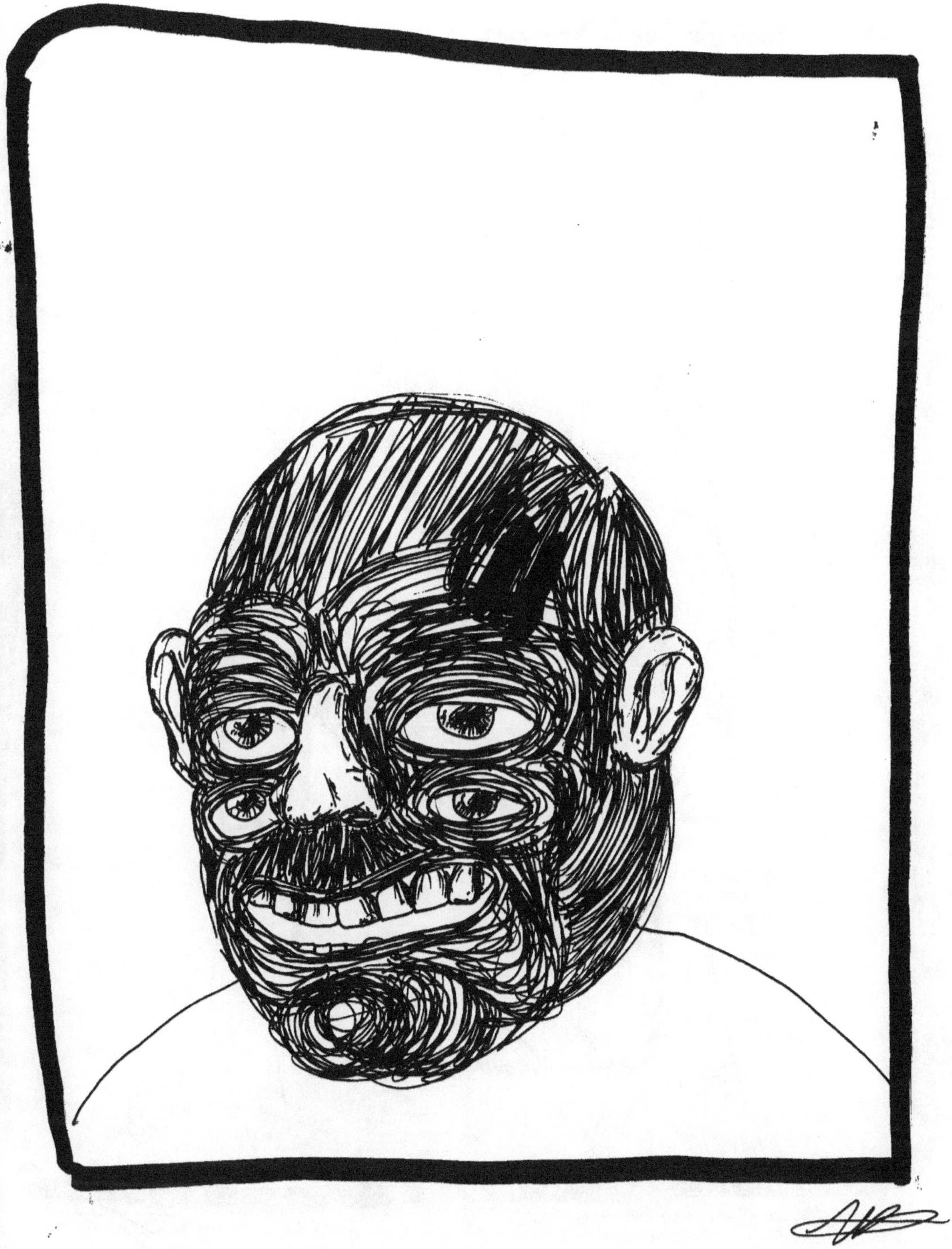

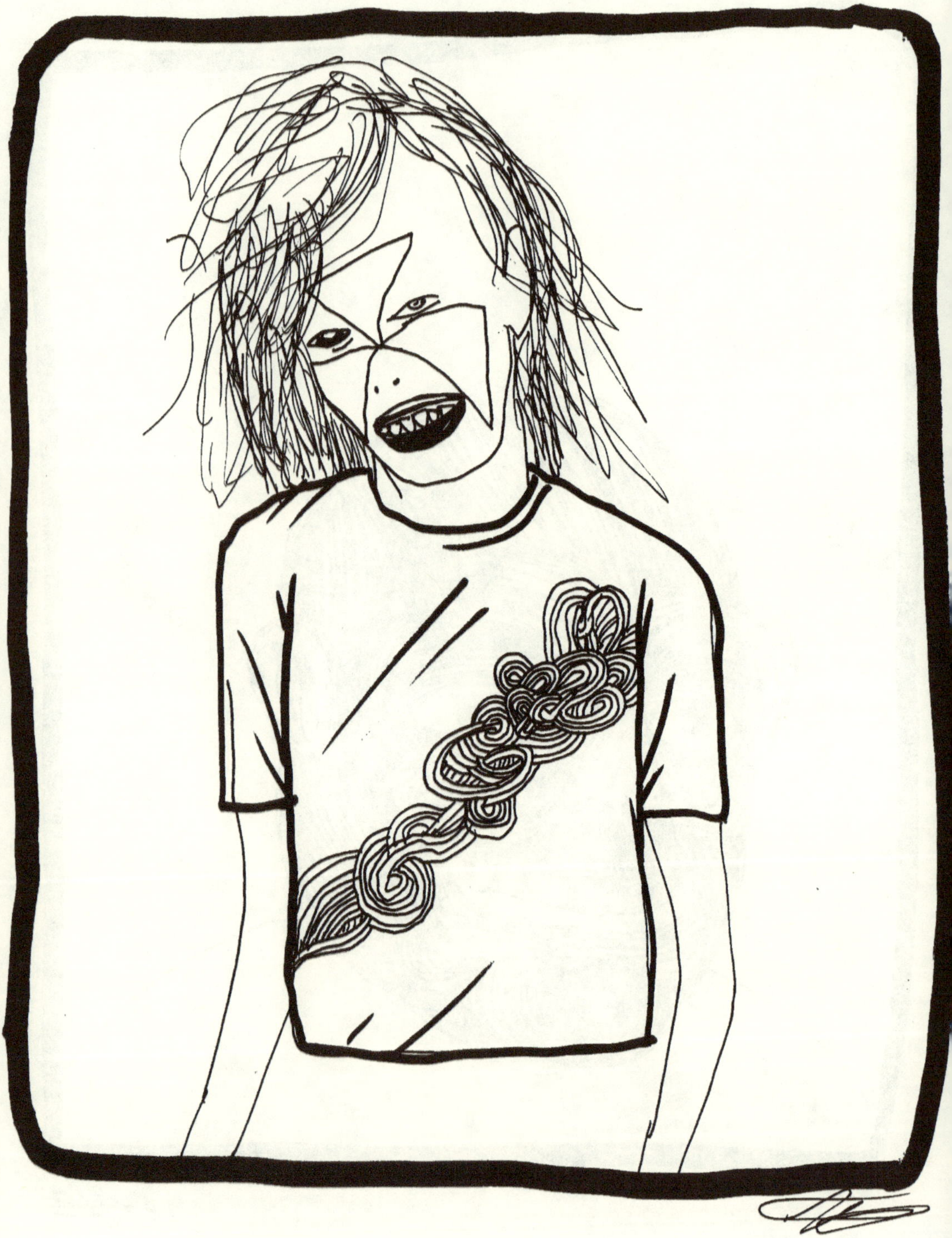

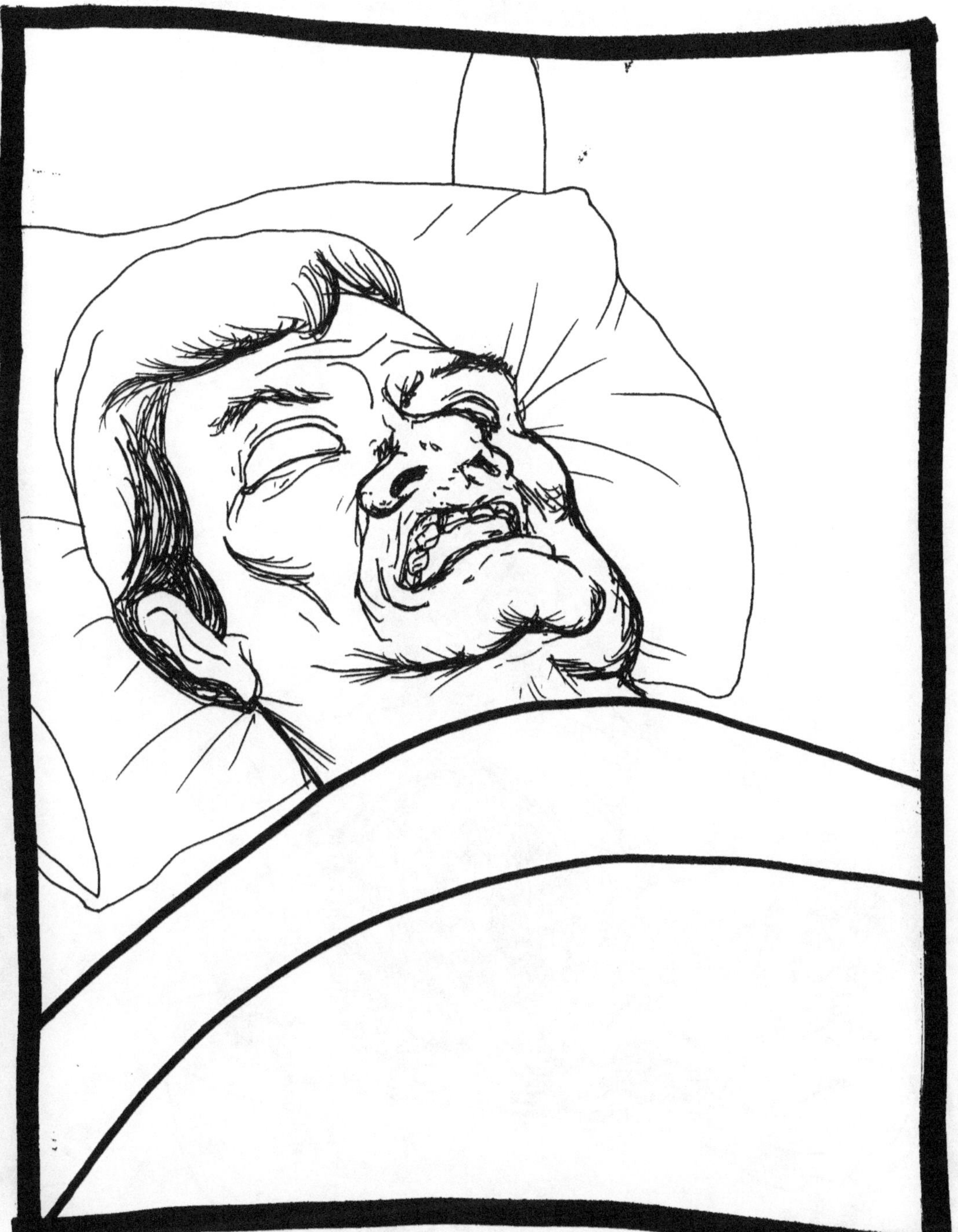

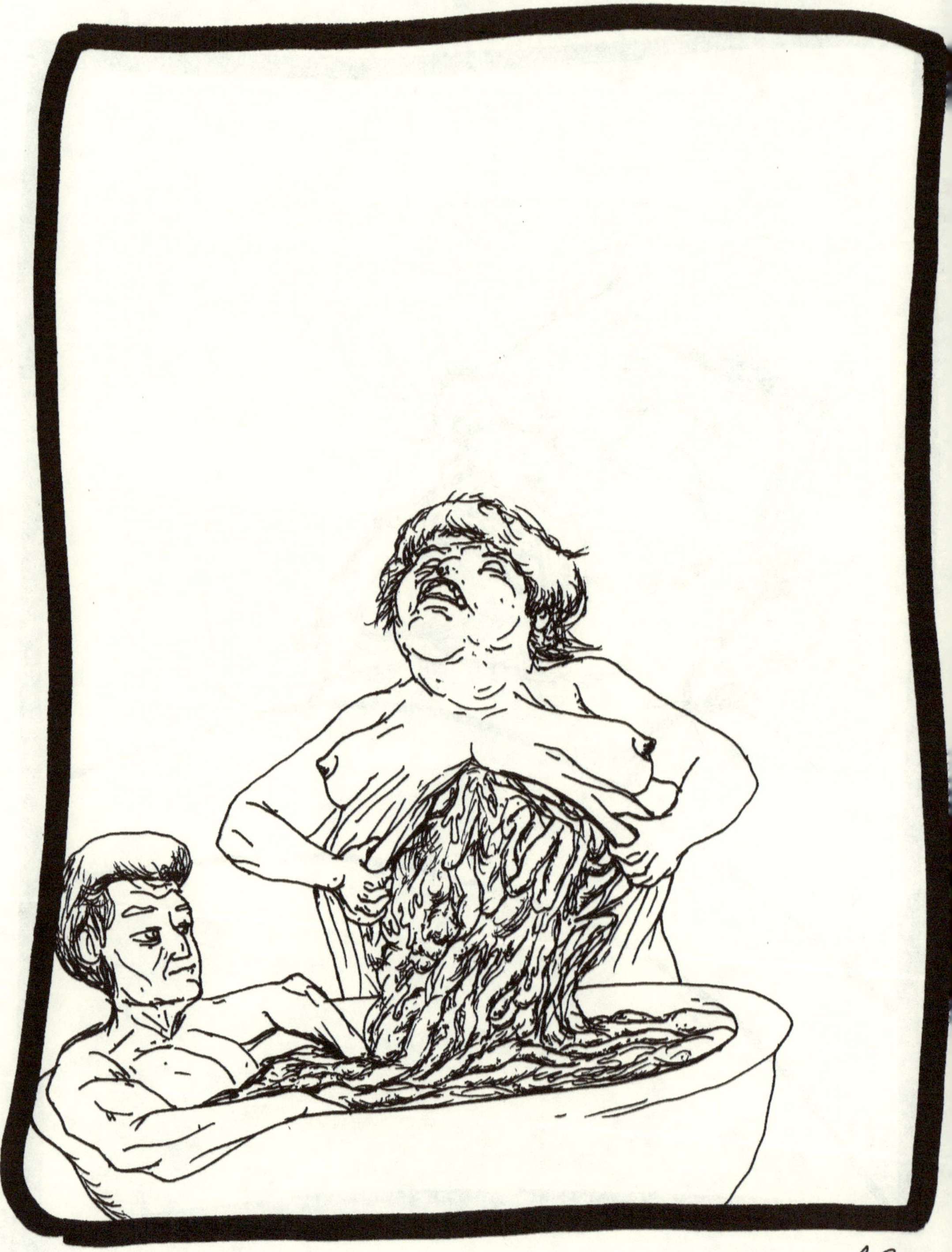

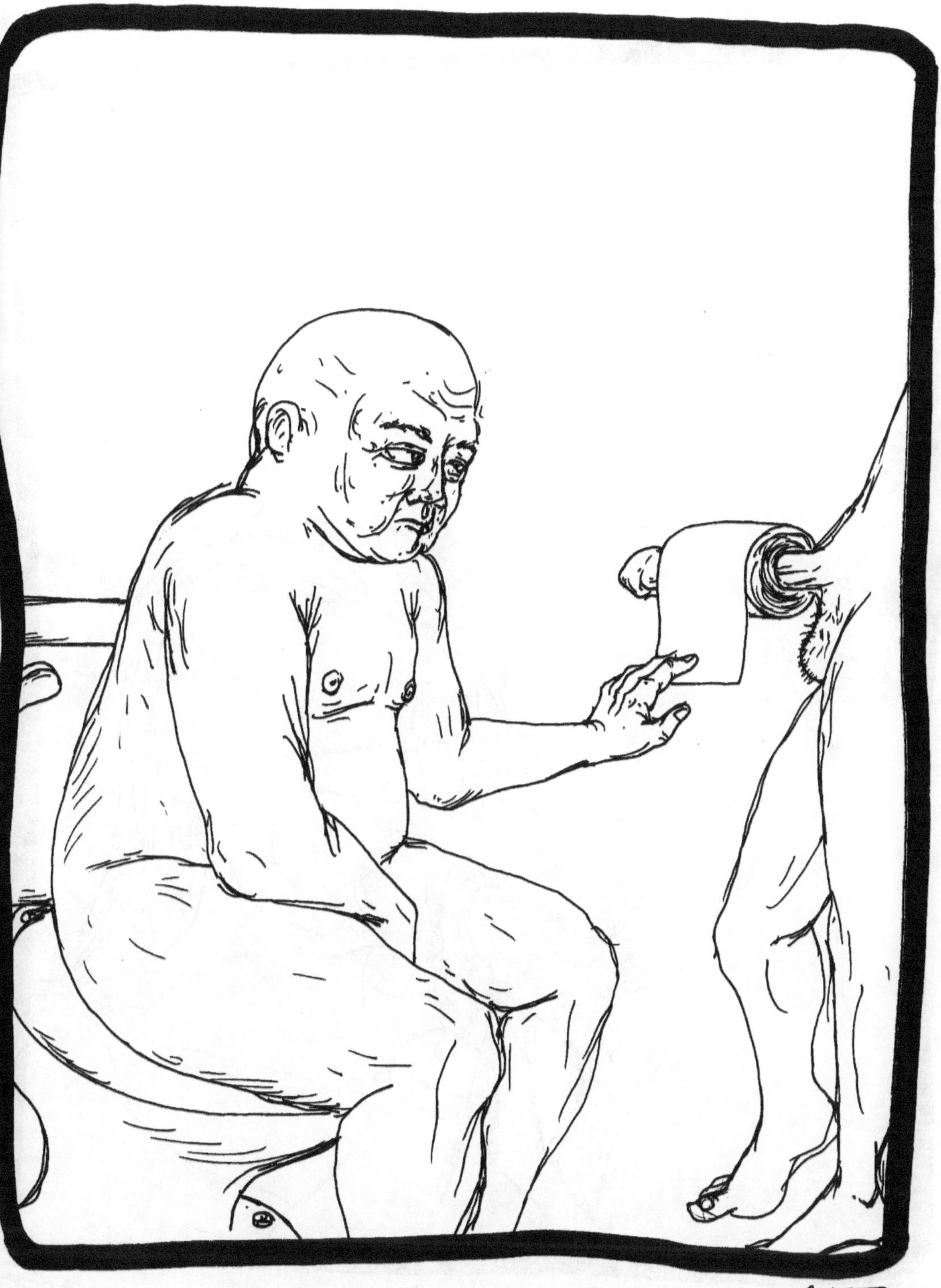

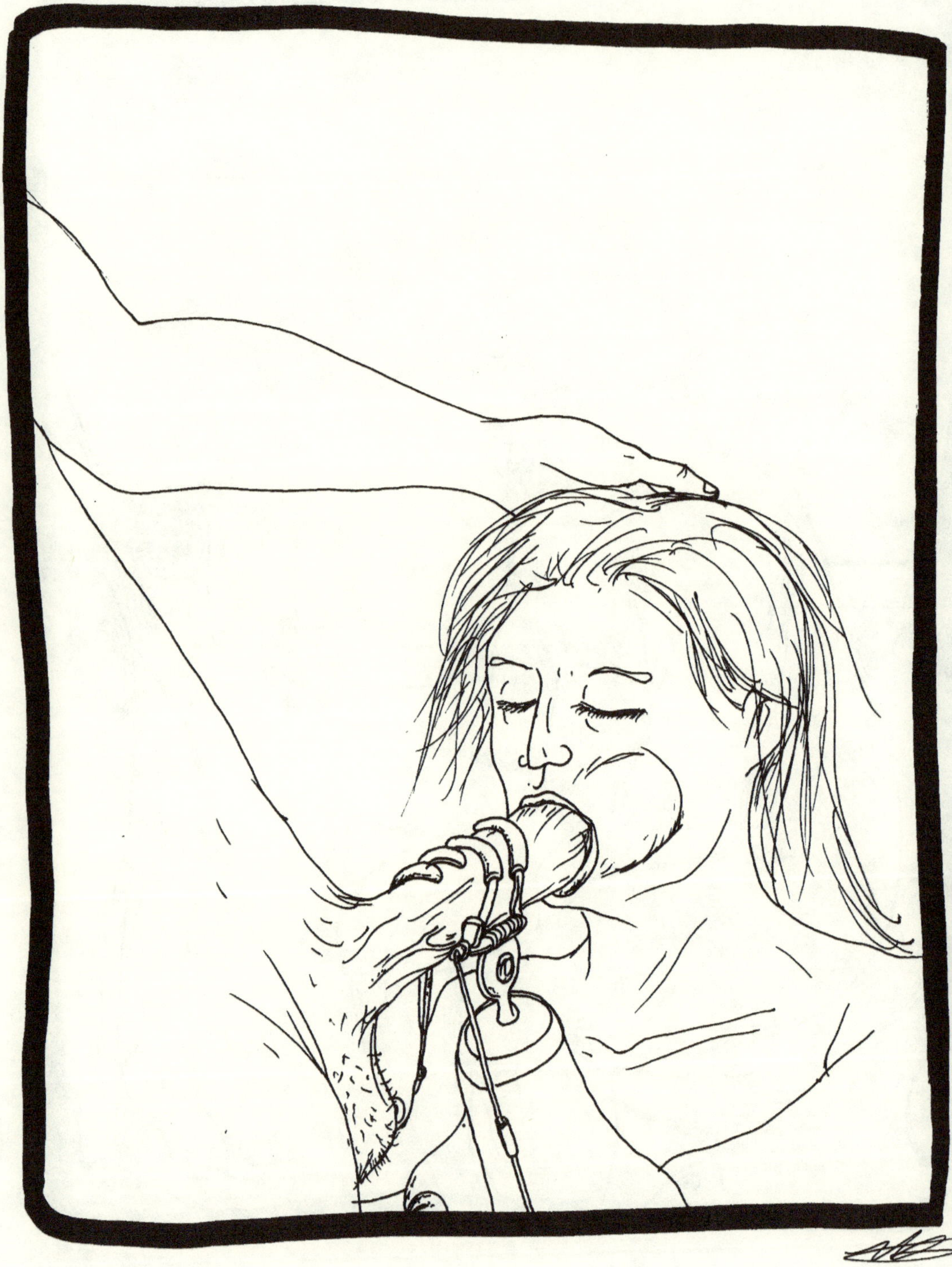

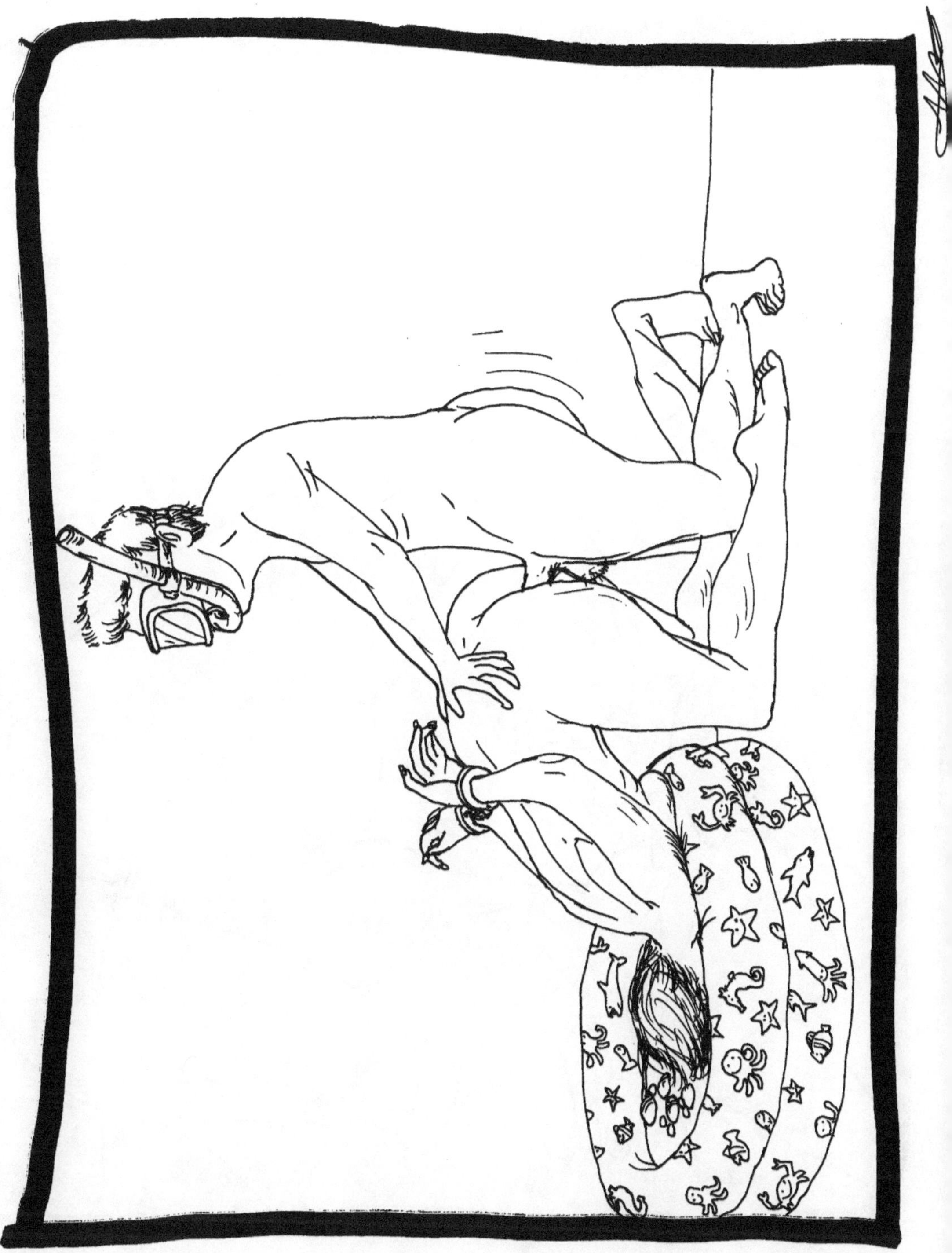

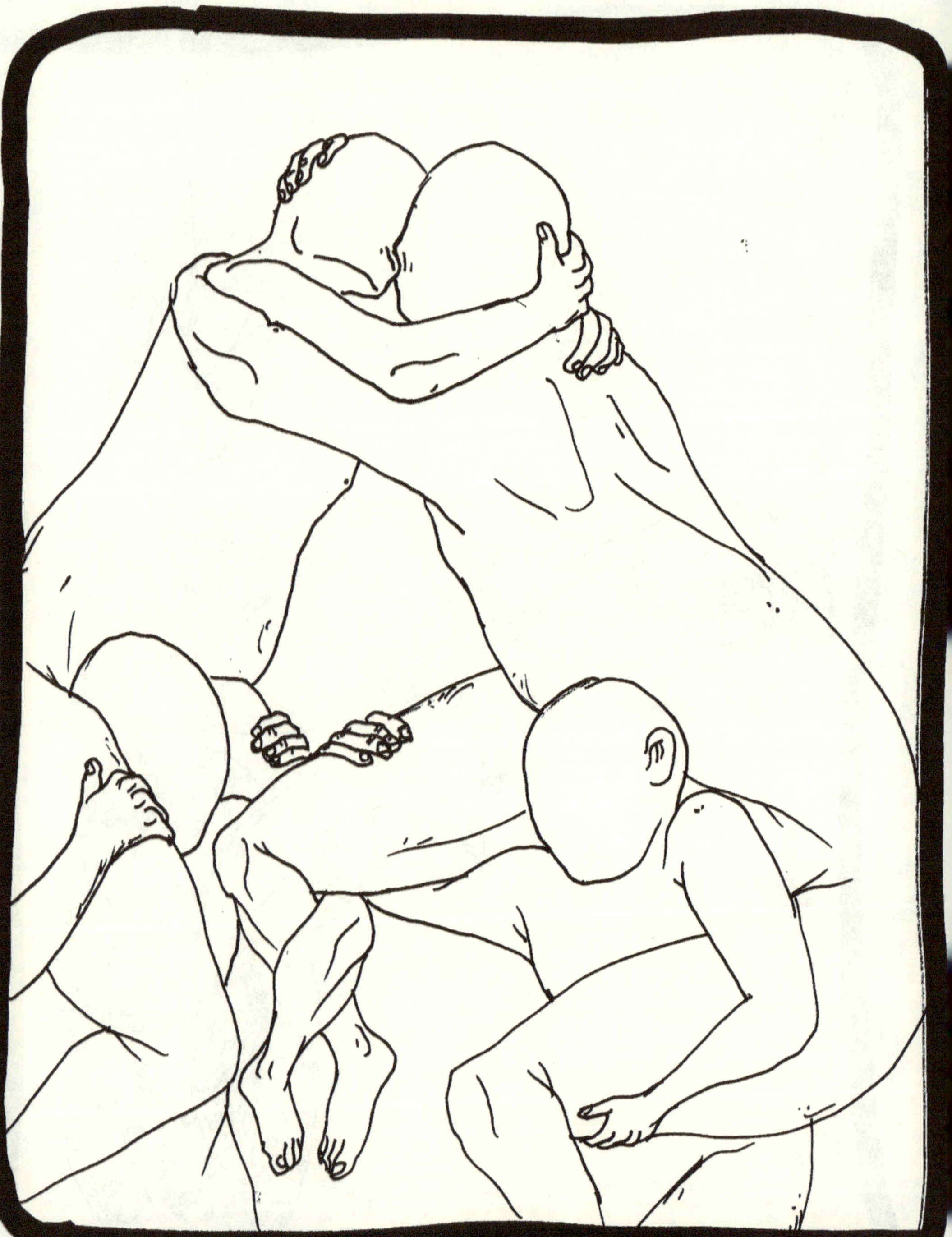

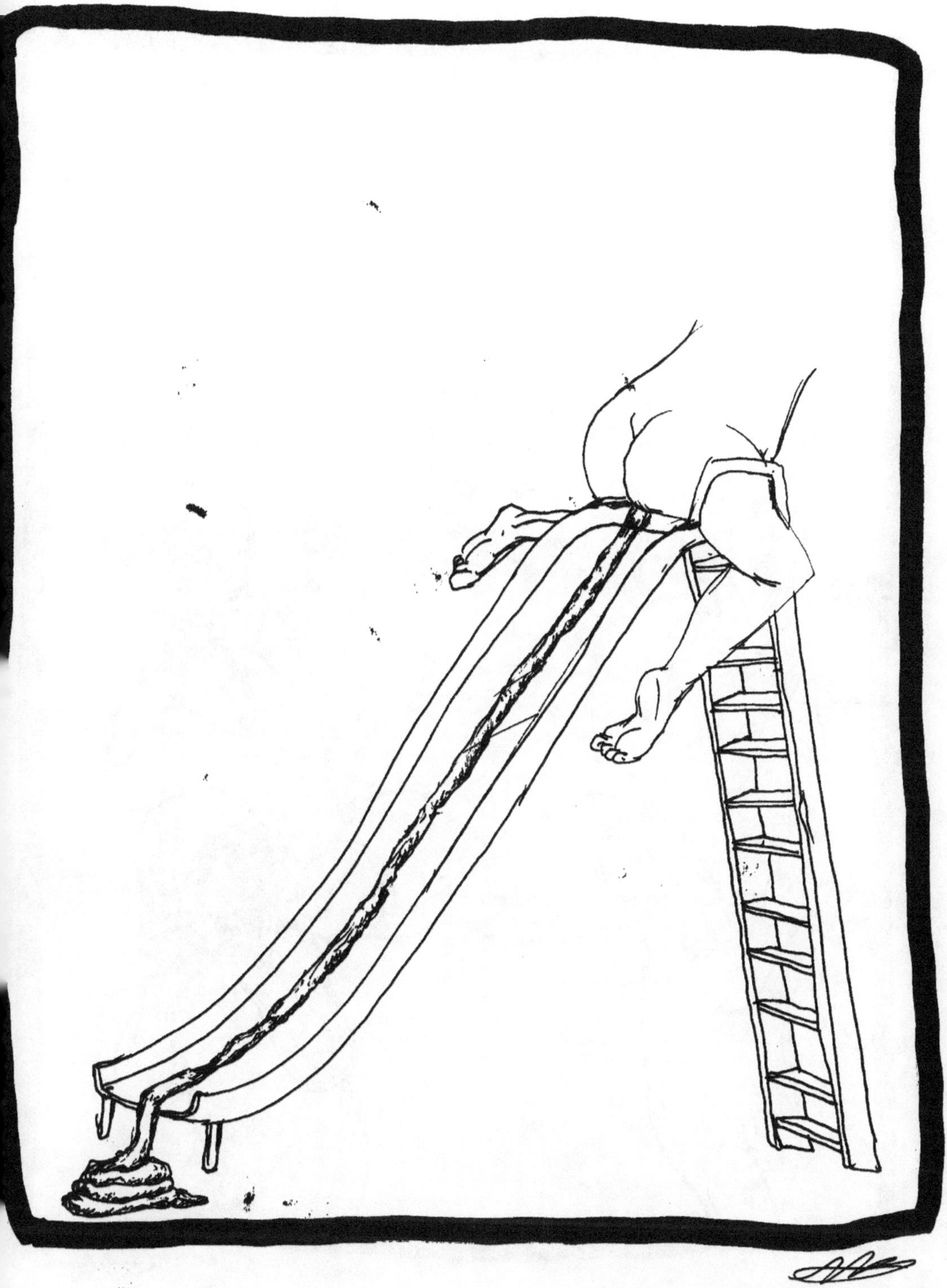

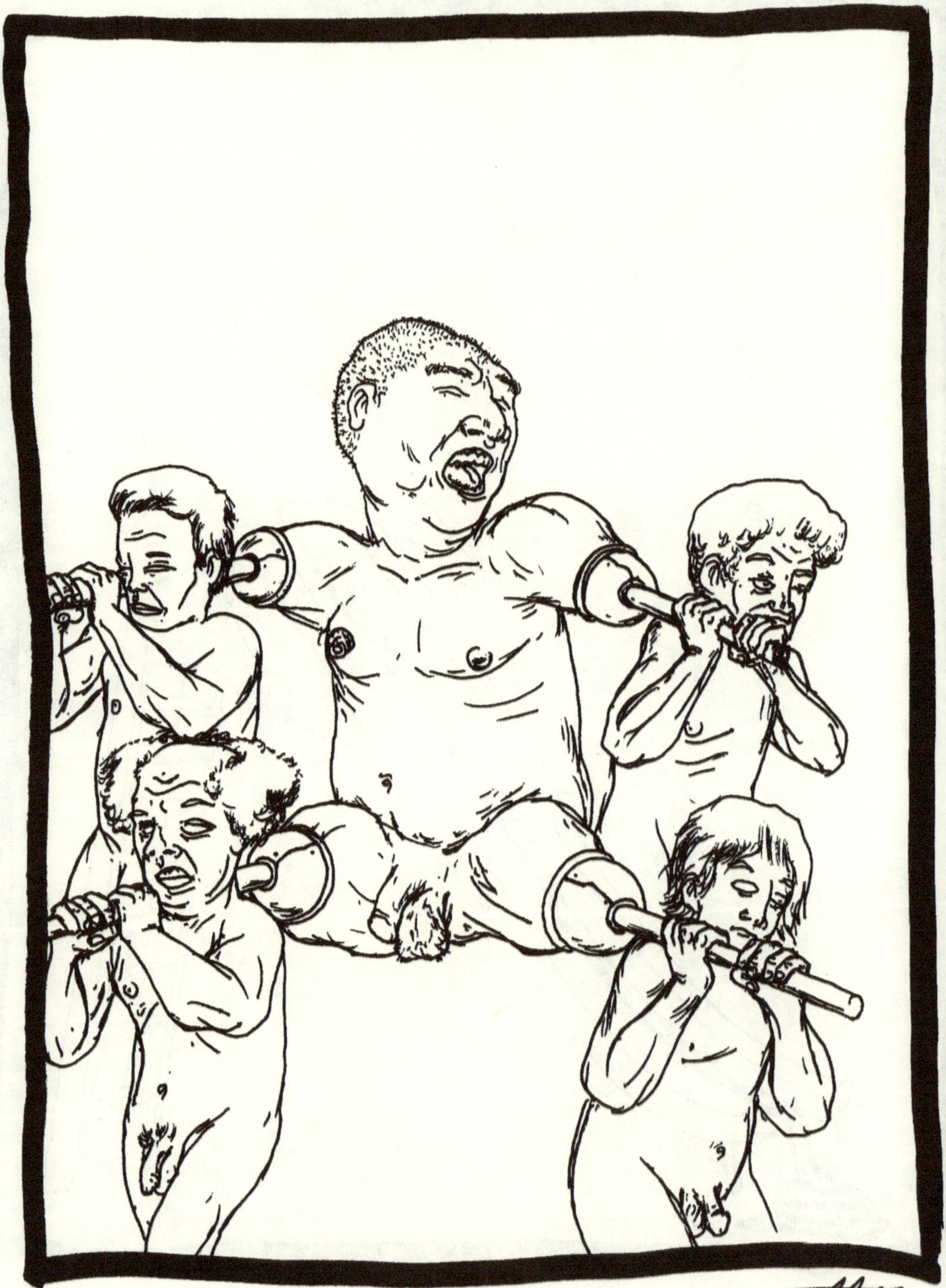

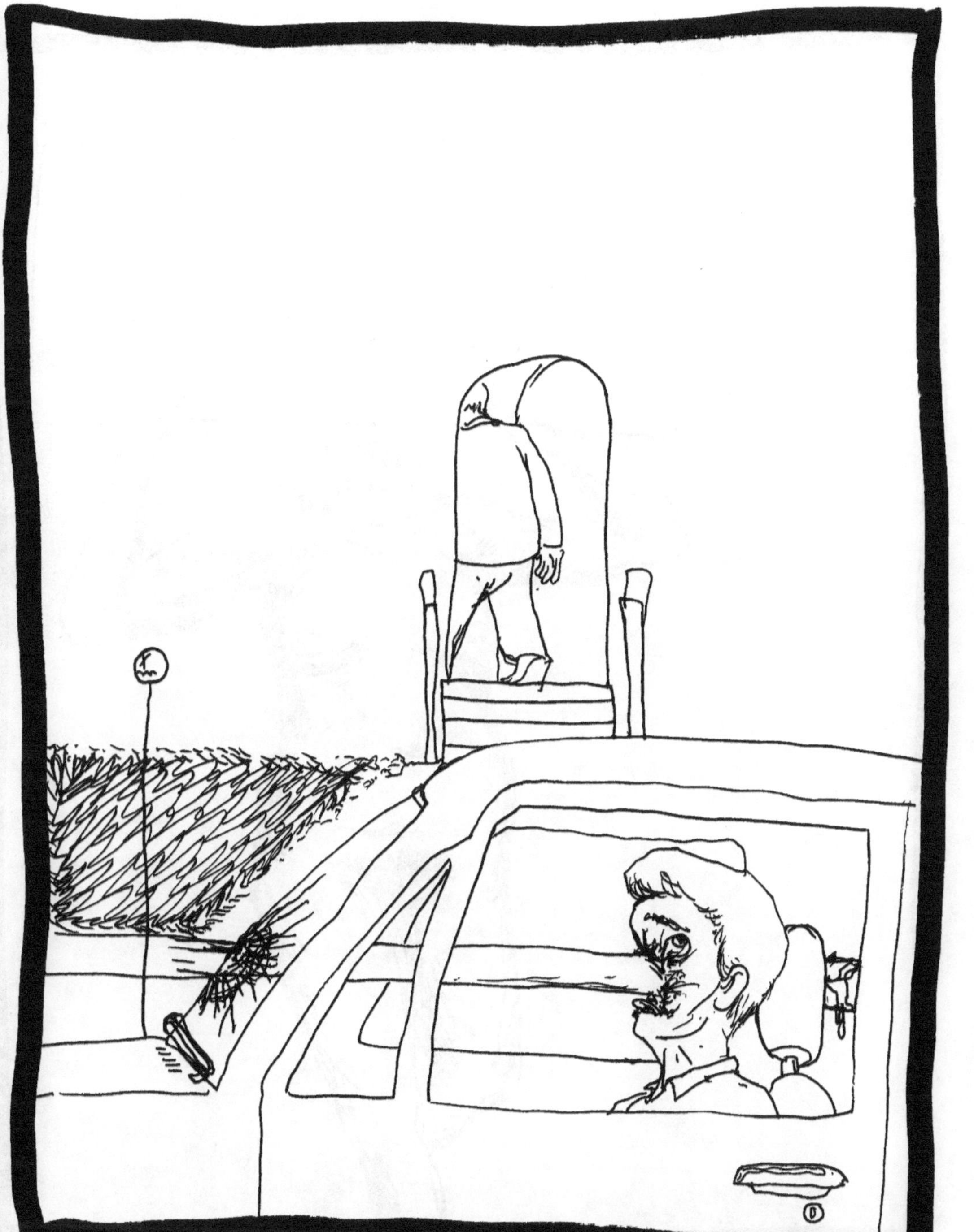

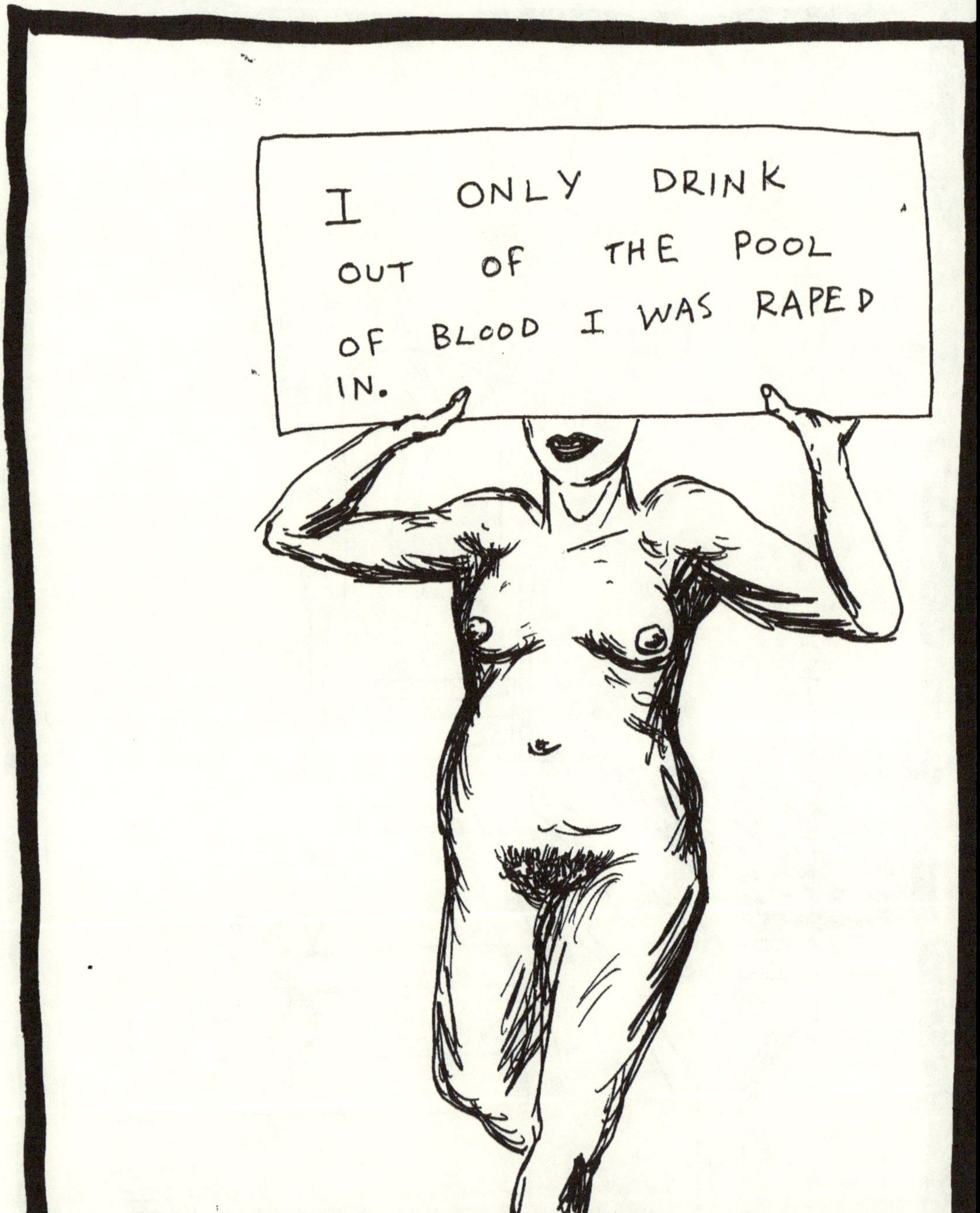
I ONLY DRINK
OUT OF THE POOL
OF BLOOD I WAS RAPED
IN.

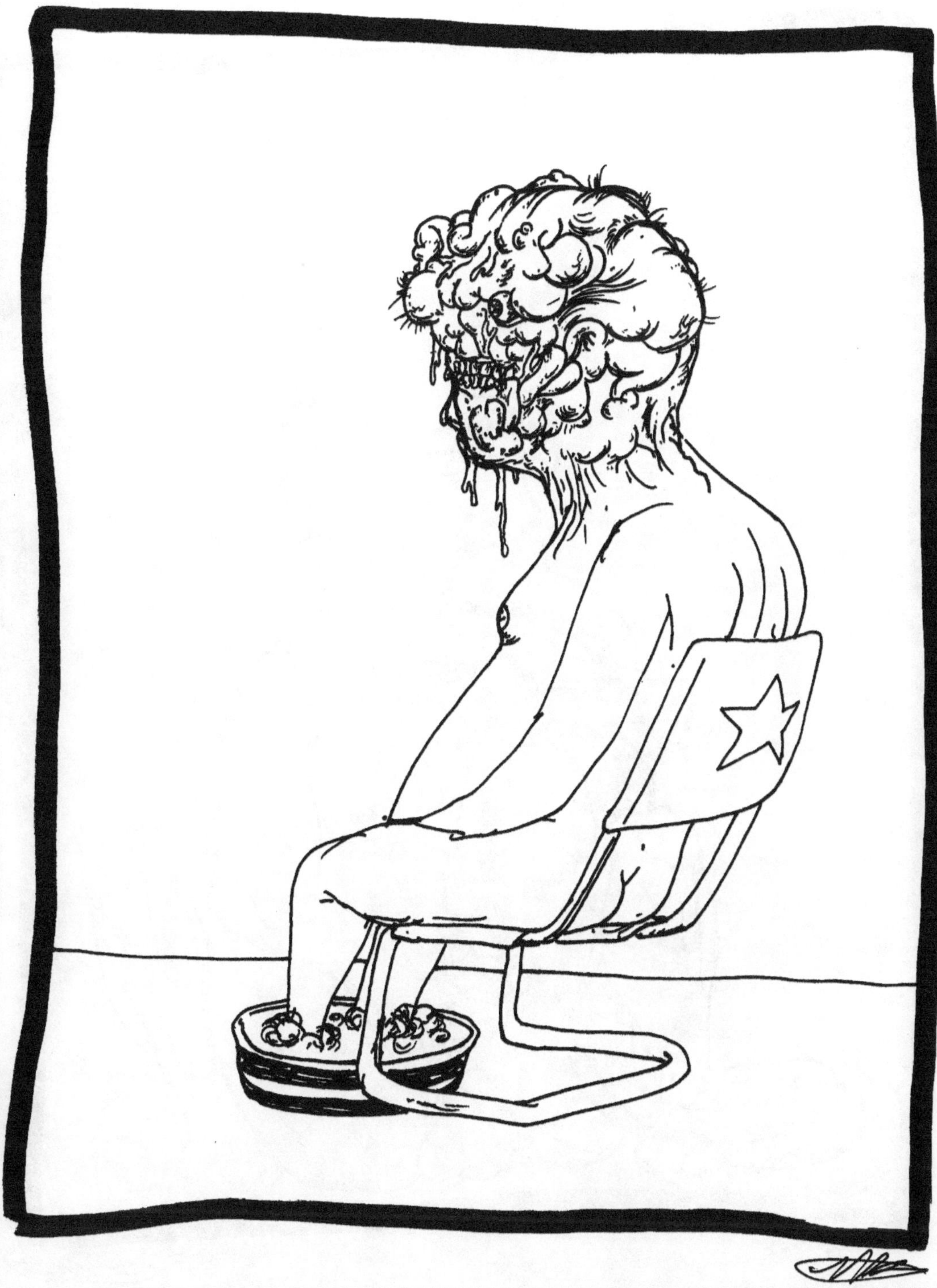

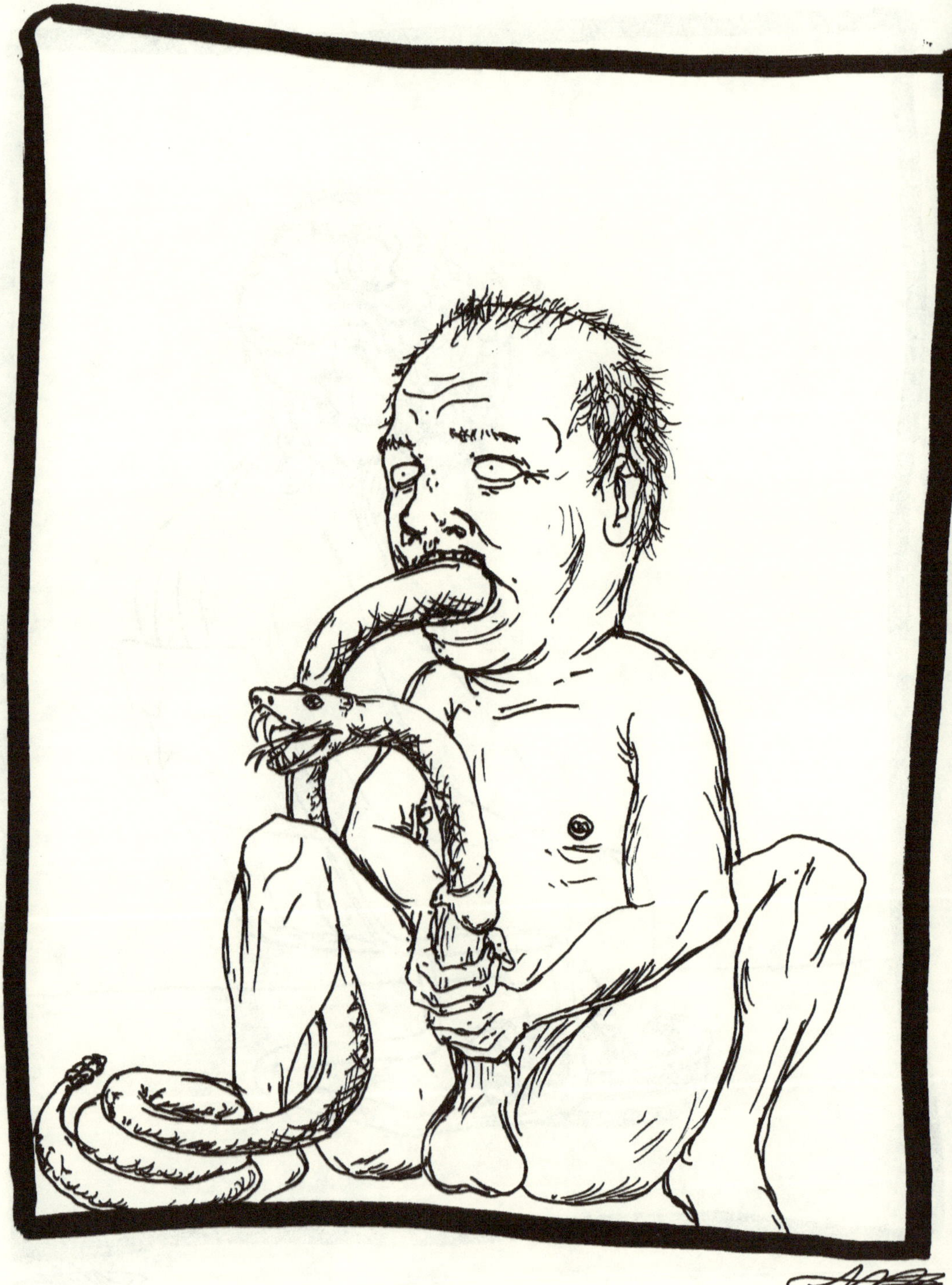

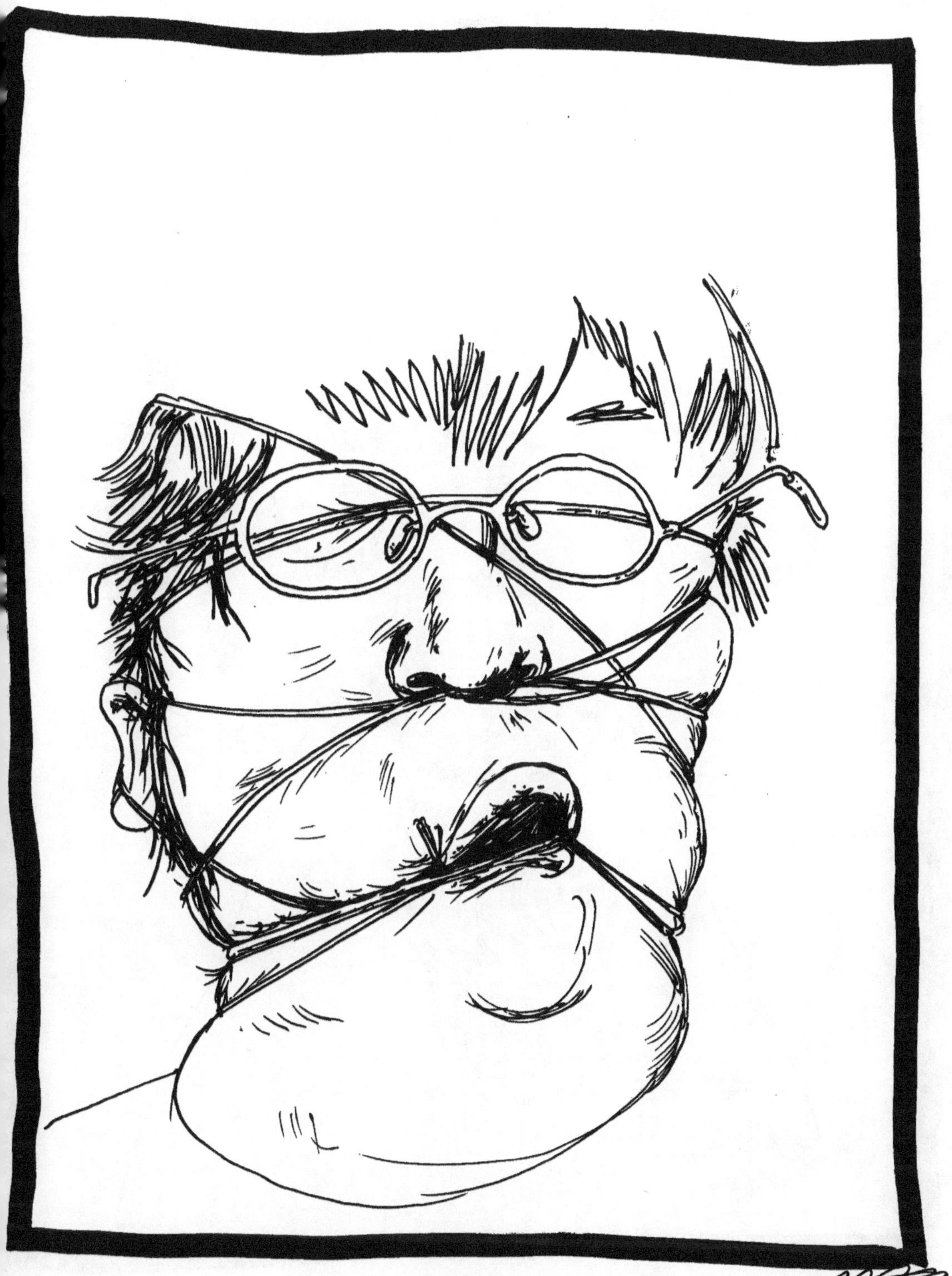

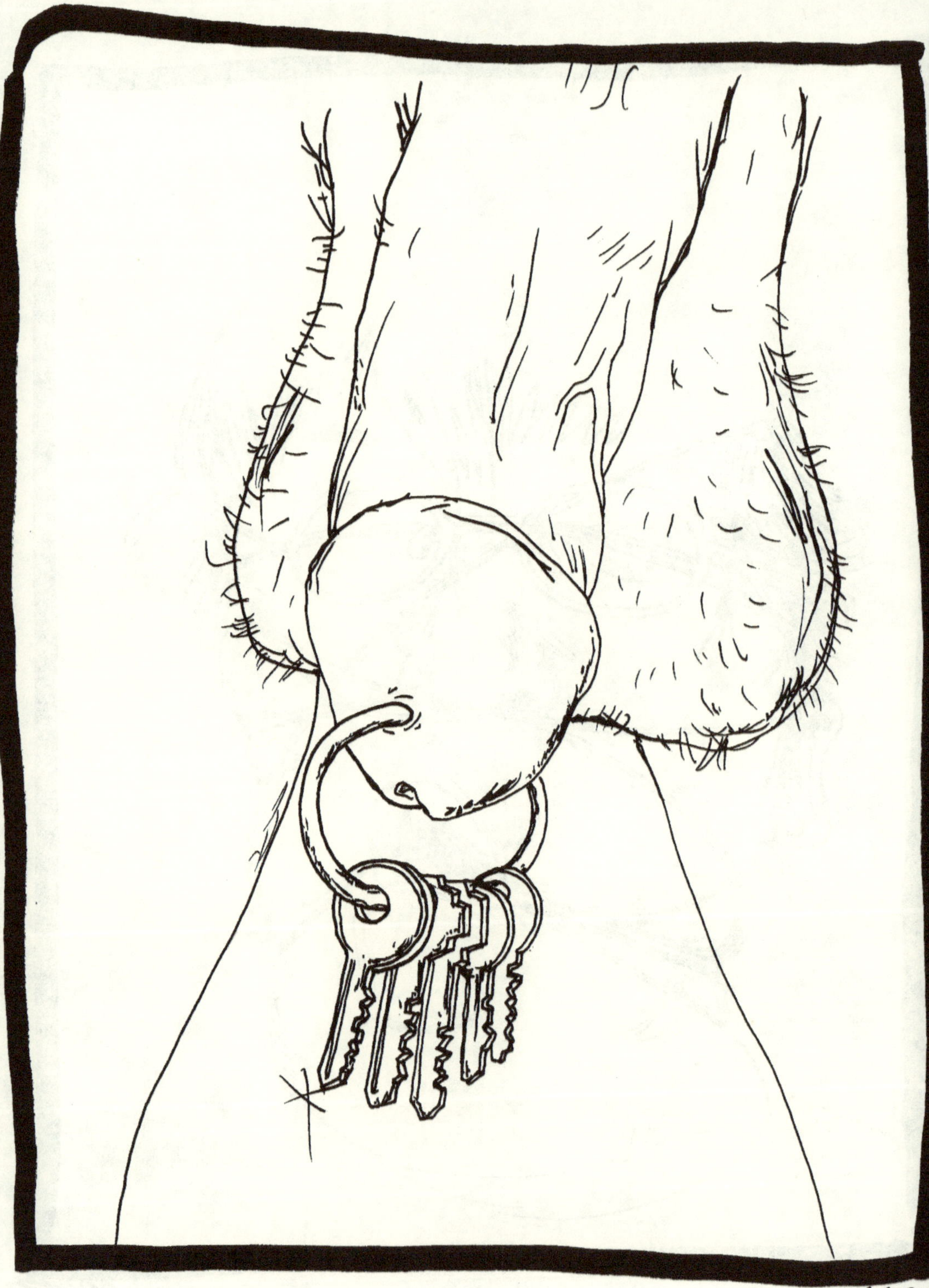

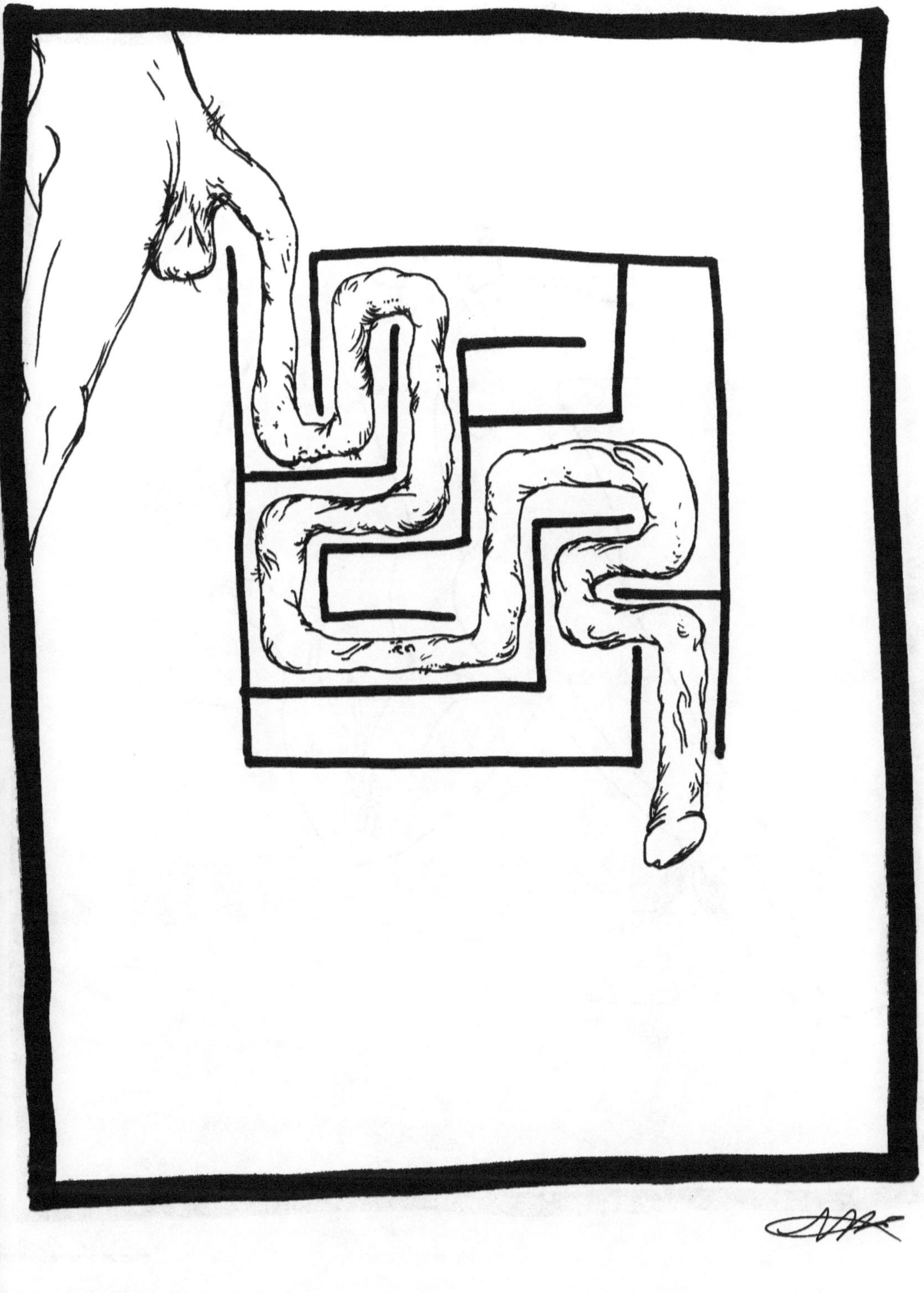

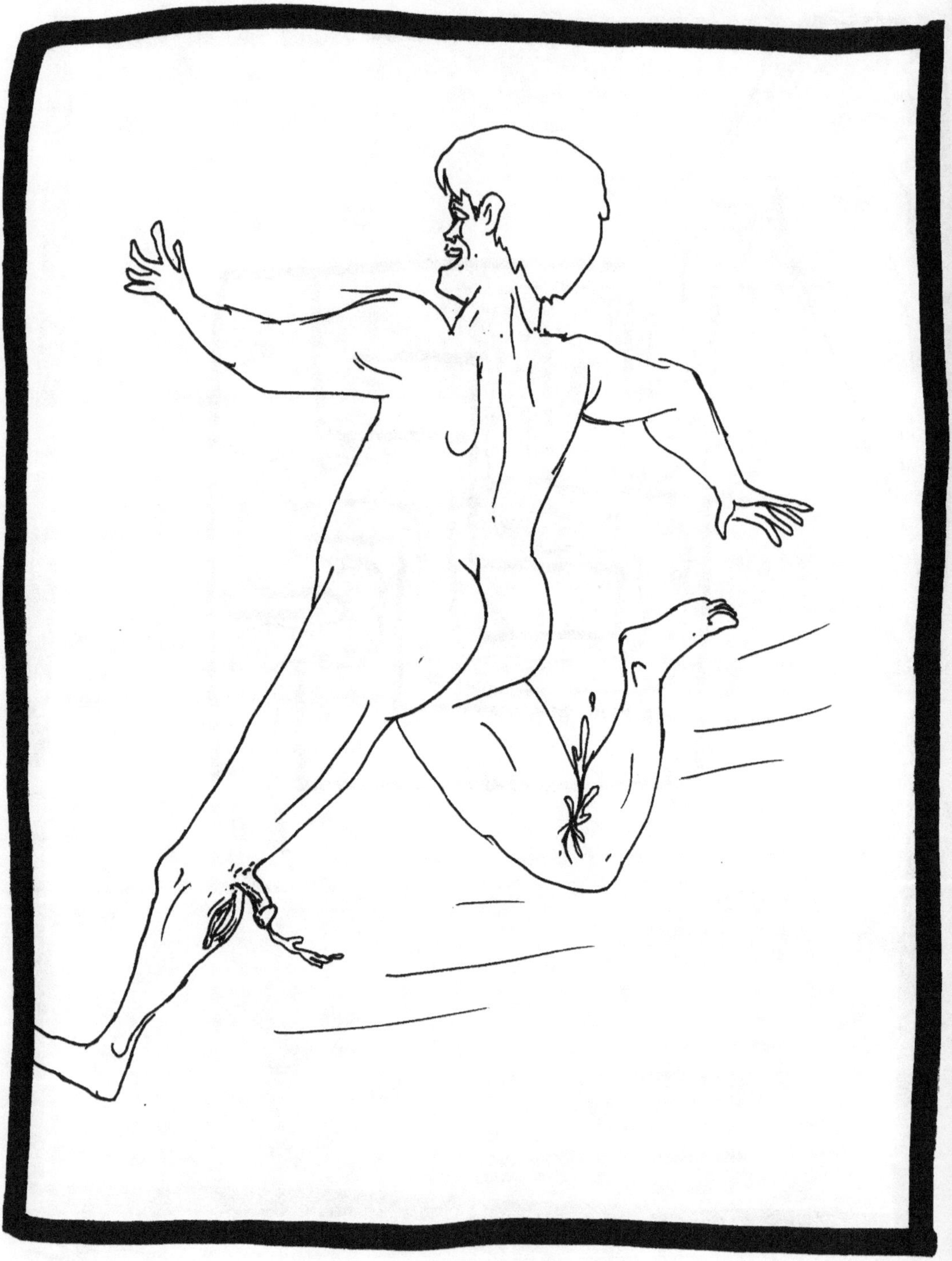

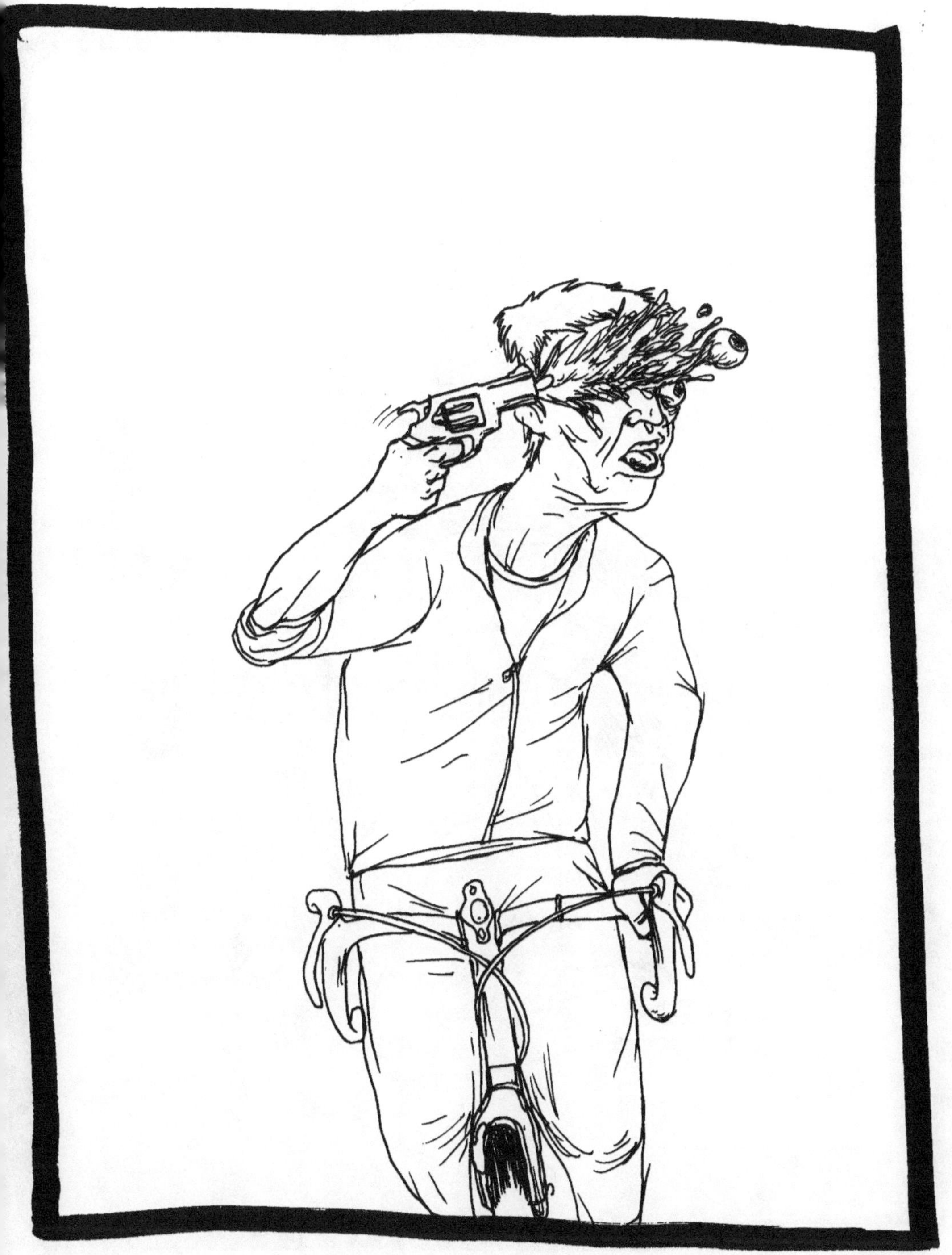

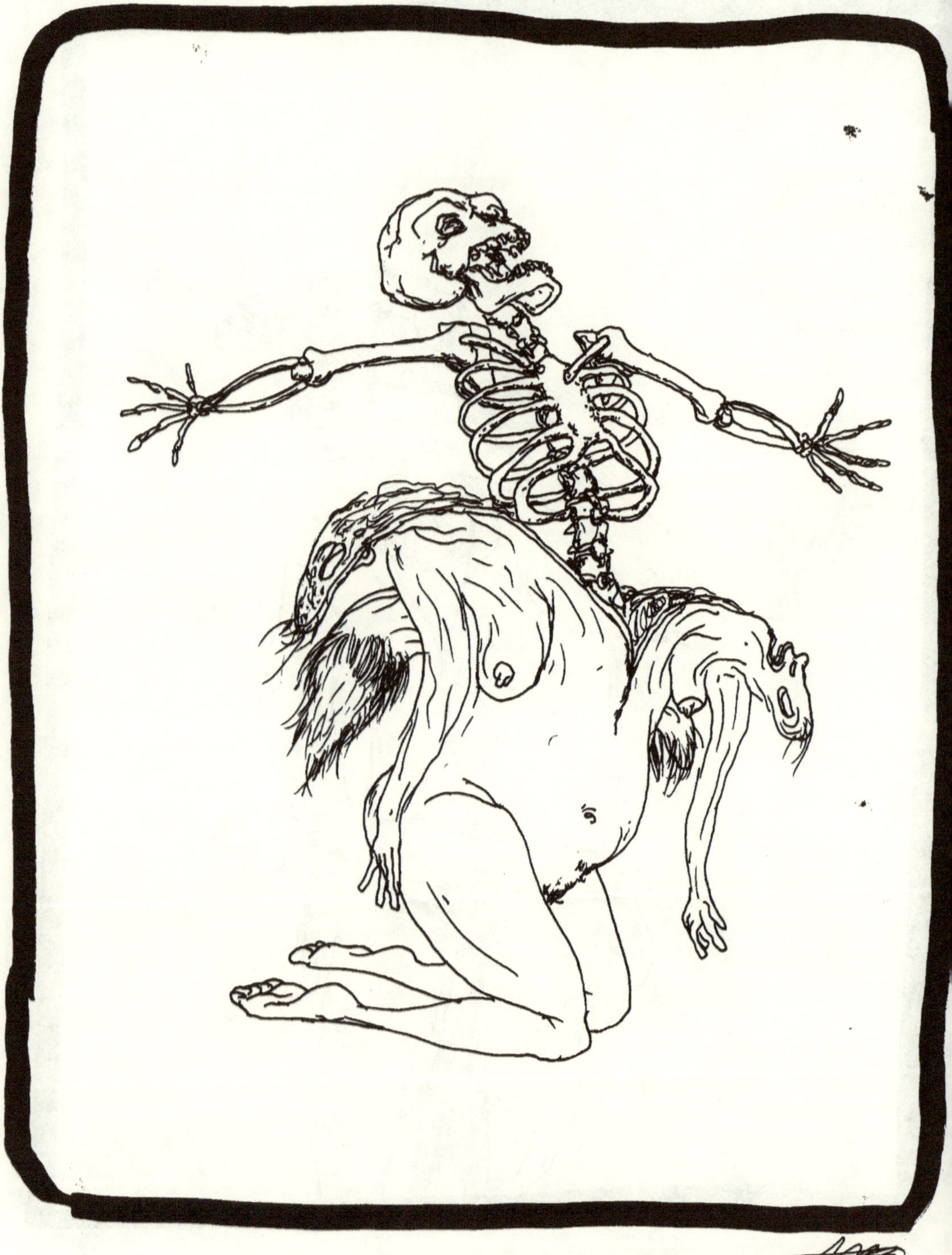

www.ingramcontent.com/pod-product-compliance
Lightning Source LLC
Chambersburg PA
CBHW022109170526
45157CB00004B/1555
9781435776166